GenXers
After God

Also by Todd Hahn and David Verhaagen
Reckless Hope

GenXers After God

Helping a Generation Pursue Jesus

Todd Hahn and David Verhaagen

with
Ellen Verhaagen
Daniel Kruidenier
and
Julie Culbreath
Phil Davis
Michael Franklin
Sean Meade
Stacy Pickerell

Baker Books

A Division of Baker Book House Co
Grand Rapids, Michigan 49516

© 1998 by Todd Hahn and David Verhaagen

Published by Baker Books
a division of Baker Book House Company
P.O. Box 6287, Grand Rapids, MI 49516-6287

Printed in the United States of America

Library of Congress Cataloging-in-Publication Data

Hahn, Todd, 1968–
    GenXers after God : helping a generation pursue Jesus / Todd Hahn and David Verhaagen.
        p.   cm.
    Includes bibliographical references.
    ISBN 0-8010-9054-7 (pbk.)
    1. Church work with young adults—United States. 2. Generation X. 3. Young adults—United States—Religious life. 4. Discipling (Christianity) 5. United States—Religion—1960– I. Verhaagen, David. II. Title.
BV4446.H345 1998
259'.25—dc21   98-10550

For information about current releases from Baker Book House, visit our web site:

http://www.bakerbooks.com

CONTENTS

5

95697

PREFACE

Douglas Coupland's *Generation X* was a book about three marginalized young adults who move to the desert and tell stories to each other. The themes resonated deeply with a generation that would come to take on the name of the novel. When one of the characters said, "Either our lives become stories, or there's just no way to get through them," we knew what she meant.[1]

Later Coupland wrote *Life after God.* Inside the dust jacket this sentence shouts: "YOU ARE THE FIRST GENERATION RAISED WITHOUT RELIGION." The book, a series of vignettes about life in a world that does not know God, ends with these words, "My secret is that I need God— that I am sick and can no longer make it alone."[2] Coupland is right. We are all sick and we can't make it on our own. We yearn for God. We need him.

This is not life after God in the sense that Coupland intended. In fact we are becoming a generation chasing after God, pursuing Jesus. This book presents a framework for those involved in the lives of GenXers—disciplers, parents, ministers, employers, and others—who want to help them grow in their faith. Building on the foundation laid in *Reckless Hope,* we present a model for helping GenXers turn their lives into stories.

This time we had lots of help from many who contributed in unique ways. It was truly a community effort. Individuals of various ages from several churches in different denominations all had a voice in shaping this material. It was a wonderful experience.

One of those people was Daniel Kruidenier. Daniel is a young man who loves God passionately. His spiritual journey has not been smooth, though. At the beginning he was fiercely angry, confused, and even despondent at times. He wrestled with difficult issues in his family and battled other problems. Through it all, he kept a journal. It was a raw, honest diary of his thoughts and intense feelings, of his desire to know God, and of his desire for integrity in his relationships. He did not write it with the intention of ever having it published. It was just his personal diary. When we asked him if we could excerpt parts of his diary to open each chapter of this book, he agreed, taking a big risk. He let us use it without conditions or attempts to edit it. These quotes are powerfully real.

Dave's wife, Ellen, has been a speaker on college campuses for more than twelve years. She is often invited to speak on the hot topic of sexual purity. Her message invariably has a powerful impact on her audience. Because it is such a vital part of each of our stories in some form, we invited her to share in chapter 12 her thoughts about helping GenXers honor God with their sexuality.

We also got some help from a group of GenXers who spent an evening with us, sharing their thoughts and experiences of growing in their faith. Julie Culbreath, Phil Davis, Michael Franklin, Sean Meade, and Stacy Pickerell all love Jesus and others well. They all speak with honesty and integrity. Their discussion concludes the book.

Jeffery Alexander, Rick Hitchcock, and Philip Prince all helped "road test" the material by participating in a discipleship group one summer. Each of them contributed powerfully to the group by sharing their hearts and lives with each other. We overflow with respect for them.

Men and women like Ken Lloyd, Cammie Hunter, David Ruff, and Bill Stauffer all gave us honest and insightful comments about some early drafts of the book. They helped shape and refine our ideas. We are grateful to all of them.

The experience of writing this book has been amazingly rich for both of us. It has helped us shape and refine some of our ideas about ministry. It has also caused us to seek out God's heart for our generation. We love being part of a generation after God.

Todd: I want to thank my colleagues and partners in ministry at Forest Hill, especially David Chadwick and Charles Overstreet, who have encouraged, supported, and created space for me to pursue a ministry to Xers both inside and outside a vibrant and way busy local church. I'm also grateful to coreX, a group of partners and friends who shape so much of my life and ministry. Sean Meade and Stacy Pickerell are more than close colleagues; Sean is a much-cherished partner and friend, and Stacy is my sister. And, most of all, I am grateful to Jane, Justin, and Jonathan, who give encouragement and sacrifice time for me to write and speak. They also give great hugs (Jane) and wet, sloppy, longed-for kisses (Justin and Jonathan). And one of them loves to be turned upside down and thrown around (Justin, not Jane, of course).

Dave: Thank you, Ellen, for being the best wife a guy could have. Thank you for being such a good mom to Christy and Abbey. I dedicate this book to you because of your commitment to ministry to this generation. Thank you, Church at Charlotte, for being our second family. Thank you to my first family and my friends for your love and commitment to me. Thank you, God, for your deep love and abundant grace.

Both of us want to thank Paul Engle at Baker Book House for his support of us and these projects. He's given us strong guidance and much encouragement.

PART 1

INTRODUCTION TO NARRATIVE DISCIPLING

A New Hunger and Thirst

We've got a generation coming up with an enormous amount of anger, frustration, confusion, and hurt. And I hate to say it but the majority of us do not have God. That means trouble. My concern is for our generation. You wanna know why crime, violence, hate, drugs, sex, counterculture is on the rise? Look at what they've done for us. Look at what they've left us. Look at how they're bringing us up. God help me and God help my generation. Please.

Living Water and Spiritual Food

Jesus is on the road. His disciples take off to get something to eat while he sits down by a well, exhausted. A woman approaches with her bucket to draw water. To most Jews like Jesus, this woman is a pariah. She is a marginalized person in their culture, yet he strikes up a conversation with her. It's about water, living water.

She has no idea what he is talking about, but he knows that she is a spiritually thirsty person.

Later his disciples return and implore him to eat something. He says, "I have food to eat that you know nothing about." Puzzled looks cross their faces. They have no idea what he is talking about, but he knows that they are spiritually hungry people (see John 4).

Food and drink. Striking images and metaphors used to speak to those who craved spiritual sustenance. Today a generation of young believers is much like those of Jesus' day. They yearn to be fed, to be nourished.

Images of food and drink abound in the culture of Generation X, that marginalized group born approximately between 1964 and 1980 who share similar attitudes and outlooks on life. Just look at the names of several bands that became popular during the adolescence of the generation: The Cranberries, Lemonheads, The Red Hot Chili Peppers, Blind Melon, Smashing Pumpkins. Also consider the GenX-targeted ad line: "Obey your thirst." These simple examples only serve to underscore that this is a hungry and thirsty group.

Preoccupation with food and drink often means that needs for nurturance and security were not satisfied in childhood. GenX's fixation with food and drink may spring from the failure to have their basic needs met. As a result they yearn to be filled up. This is not only true emotionally, but spiritually as well. This generation has a healthy spiritual appetite.

New Challenges in Making Disciples

This spiritual hunger drives many GenXers to seek out mystical experiences, developing their own unique religious faith. In spite of this, many will come into an authentic relationship with Jesus, particularly if the church rises to the challenges posed by this generation. In *Reckless Hope* we detailed these challenges and highlighted the important themes and strategies that are necessary to reach this unique group with the timeless gospel.

Once we bring these individuals into the kingdom of God, however, we must mentor and disciple them in their faith. Author Douglas Coupland calls this "the first generation raised without religion." If this is so, discipling this generation of new believers is an exciting and sobering task.

Our charge is to highlight the important concepts and themes that we believe are important in spiritually mentoring this generation. We believe that they are different from older generations in several important areas that have bearing on discipling relationships. We draw these differences from research, interviews, media, analysis of cultural trends, and personal experiences in discipling.

Clearly these differences are not true of every member of GenX. We will speak of fragmented families, but many have loving, intact Christian families. Many have been well-taught in their homes and churches, but many have not, and the differences mentioned here are characteristic of the challenges that face those who move into discipling relationships with members of Generation X. We argue that even GenXers who come from loving, intact families and solid church backgrounds were raised in a culture that is fundamentally different than it was just a generation ago.

What's So Different about This Generation?

Every generation is different from the ones before it. The constantly changing social context cannot help but

15

influence and shape each new group as it grows and matures. The same is true for GenX. There are many similarities with previous generations at the same age; however, there are also many striking differences. Here are some important differences in faith, hope, and love that may have direct impact on our attempts to disciple members of GenX.

Differences in Faith

In the middle of a college Bible study on Jesus' claim to be the only way to God, the leader made a comment that other religions were false and did not offer the same hope as Christianity. A member of the group was clearly dismayed by the statement. She said sternly, "That's just your opinion. I think it's okay to believe in Jesus, but that doesn't mean that other people's religions are wrong."

In *The Closing of the American Mind*, Allan Bloom argues that the one guarantee that any college professor now has when he stands before a classroom is that nearly all of his young students believe that truth is relative.[1] To most members of GenX, truth is completely subjective; it is within the realm of opinion. Something is "true" only insofar as it is "true" for each individual. The notion of objective or absolute truth is largely lost to this generation.

GenXers almost invariably see no other option to subjective reality. One claiming to know some "absolute truth" runs the risk of being considered a fanatic at best or a bigot at worst. This view of relative truth invariably translates to an emphasis on subjective, mystical experiences or what we call "cut and paste" faith. Cut and paste faith involves cutting the desirable tenets from various systems of belief and pasting them together to form your own creed. Douglas Coupland calls this "Me-ism." He defines it as "a search by an individual, in the absence of training in traditional religious tenets, to for-mulate a personally tailored religion by himself. Most frequently a mishmash of reincarnation, personal dia-logue with a nebulously defined god figure, naturalism, and karmic eye-for-eye attitudes."[2]

For example, one young caller to a radio talk show claimed to be a "born-again Christian" and a "practic-ing Buddhist," even though the doctrines of grace and karma are diametrically opposed. Even GenXers who grew up in the church and have received good teaching tend to cut and paste their faith, dismissing with ease bothersome doctrines and troubling tenets.

If the church is successful in reaching GenX, we must be prepared to spiritually mentor and disciple these in-dividuals, anticipating their tendency to overemphasize the mystical or cut and paste their beliefs. For the most part, we must expect that GenXers will have differences in how they approach their faith. These differences rep-resent formidable challenges in discipling relationships.

There has already been plenty of discussion about the short attention span of this, the MTV generation. They are used to rapidly changing images, upbeat presenta-tion, and a barrage of information. Consequently they are able to take in huge amounts of data in a short amount of time; they thrive on being carpet bombed with facts.

This, too, presents challenges for spiritual mentor-ing. It causes us to rethink our approach to discipling. How should we teach? Should we go through a book to-gether? What about memorizing Scripture? How do we teach this generation to pray? GenXers may soak up in-formation quickly, but how do we help them think crit-ically about spiritual matters?

Differences in Hope

One GenXer, a believer and recent college graduate, said, "I'd like to get established in my career and then get married but I don't want to have kids. To be honest, I'd actually love to have children but I just don't think it's fair to raise a kid in this world with the shape it's in. Things are already pretty bad, but by the time my kids would grow up, it will be a disaster."

GenXers are individually hopeful but corporately hopeless. If you ask a member of Generation X about his life, he is likely to express a sense of hope. He will be hopeful about finishing school, getting a good job, getting married, and maybe even raising kids. But when you ask about "big-picture hope," the kind of hope that is secure in the belief that God is firmly in control and weaving events together with a clear purpose, you will usually get a different response.

For GenXers, the world has simply spun too far out of control. It has gotten too big, too unmanageable. It is unpredictable and chaotic. One young GenXer stated proudly that his religion was "randomness." Life is a series of random, unconnected events. What a frightening thought!

Baby Boomers grew up with the sense that they could change the world; GenXers have no such inclination. They believe that they can manage their own lives and perhaps have an impact at the local, grassroots level, but they have no illusions of having dramatic, global impact. The world, as they see it, is going from bad to worse. It is ripping apart at the seams, exploding into a million fragments.

The reality, however, is that God is in control. Instead of the world ripping apart at the seams, God is knitting it all together, weaving a masterful tapestry. Instead of creation exploding into a million fragments, God is summing it all up in Christ, gluing it all back together.

18

On one level, the condition of the world is deteriorating and may even continue to worsen. On another level, however, God is already at work putting broken things back together. One day it will be complete as "all things" are restored and brought together under Jesus' authority (see Acts 3:21; Eph. 1:9–10).

Imparting this understanding of what God is doing in the world is vitally important in our discipling relationships. It has implications for how GenX will approach such things as evangelism and missions. Even more fundamentally, it has dramatic impact on each GenXer's view of the character of God.

The challenge in discipling GenX is to move them beyond superficial, personal hopefulness and into a deep, abiding hope that God is moving in the world and he is up to something good. The writer of Hebrews calls this kind of hope "an anchor for the soul, firm and secure" (Heb. 6:19). This can be the hope of Generation X.

Differences in Love

This generation's well-documented experiences with divorce, child abuse, and domestic violence have caused them to be largely disconnected from others. Many struggle with the legacy that their parents have given them—difficulty with commitment, intimacy, and relational integrity. Some do not know how to relate well; others simply keep their emotional distance. This is not to say that many do not have significant, deep relationships. They clearly do, but as a generation they do not understand others well. They have difficulty in family relationships, dating relationships, and friendships.

"It's hard for me to think of God as a loving Father when my own father was anything but loving," says one young woman, a graduate student. Similar words are expressed by many other GenXers. Growing up in chaotic families with absent or even abusive fathers has left its mark on the generation's concept of God. Worship a heavenly *Father*? It's more difficult for many GenXers than most would believe. They need relationships with more mature believers who guide them into intimacy with a good Father.

Even for those coming from relatively stable families, we would expect that the first postmodern generation would not have a full sense of God's character. How can you love God when you do not know him? ~~GenX disciples need spiritual mentors who help ground them in a knowledge of God.~~

Relationships with parents are vitally important to GenX. Many GenXers still live at home with their parents into their middle or even late twenties. According to the U.S. Census Bureau, 73 percent of men aged 18–24 were living with their parents or other relatives. The proportion of men and women aged 25–34 living at home with their parents has doubled since 1970. This challenges the notion that permanently moving out of the home at age eighteen, either to go to college or to marry, is the norm. For Generation X, it clearly is not. Even many who do go off to college return home after graduating or dropping out. Being an adult in your own parents' home is difficult and full of complexity. GenXers must determine how to live with their parents in a way that honors them and God.

Having been raised in a hypersexual culture, GenXers have also paid the price in their relationships with members of the opposite sex. They have a warped view of intimacy. Young adults have wrestled with their sexuality since time immemorial. However, our culture has become so deeply imbued by sexuality that even the most godly young person is likely to be bombarded with sexual images, talk, and ideologies. For the most part, GenXers have never been exposed to God's view of sexuality. They neither know healthy sexual boundaries nor understand what God's intent was in creating those boundaries.

GenXers need a new view of love and relationships. The discipling relationship itself can model relational depth and integrity. In that context GenXers can be taught about the character of God. They can learn how to love others well. They can hear about God's design for healthy sexuality. They can discover how to live in a community of believers.

Timeless Similarities

Despite the differences in their faith, hope, and love, this generation has many timeless similarities with previous generations. Like generations before them, GenXers have a deep spiritual hunger. They thirst for God. They crave connection with others. In many ways the generation's hunger and thirst are more salient, more obvious than they were in past generations.

Despite this, it is not likely that GenXers will seek out spiritual mentors. Those interested in discipling them need to move toward them in relationship, not pushing too hard or coming on too strong. GenXers need time to establish trust. Once the relationship has been established, disciplers may be both invigorated and frustrated. There may be passionate discussion and radical thinking, but the old ideas and behaviors are often intractable.

At the core, GenXers hunger and thirst for satisfying relationships with God and others. This is nothing new, and spiritual mentors can help them discover and experience true faith, hope, and love in a new way. We call it narrative discipling.

The Story of Our Lives

I sit in my room. Got everything. Nice clothes, collectibles, music, bed, desk, chair, fishing stuff. I live in a nice house, get to work out, have plenty of friends, know God. Let me out. This person called Daniel should be happy. I feel like I should be miles below the surface locked in a cage. Daniel should be happy, must be happy. I'm not. Why not? I'm not supposed to be here. First came anger. Anger swells up greater than life. One person with anger like mine could take on ten men without. It's an inner anger. Makes me quiet. Makes me slow, makes me blank, with an expressionless expression. Loss of motivation. I lost it, can't find it. Feel like I don't need it. People say work hard, try hard, fight for right. End result for everyone: death. Everyone gets there eventually. Life's hard.

On and off depression, total lack of motivation and inability to try is all part of my life right now. How long will it last? I know it won't last forever. And I know God has a perfect plan set up in the long run. I guess that's the answer.

Living in Stories

We cannot overstate the importance of story in our lives. As sleepy children, we long to be told good-night stories by our parents. If our parents are wise, they tell us stories of valorous little boys and brave little girls, of elves and trolls and little pigs, of good fairies and wicked witches. Stories form the texture of our childhood. As adolescents, we thrill to the stories of ballerinas and intrepid teenage detectives. As adults, we may cling to the stories of sports stars, rags-to-riches business successes, or, in our less imaginative moments, celebrities and soap opera stars.

As we grow older, we tell stories with increasing frequency, often to the chagrin of younger generations. "I remember when . . ." may sound to a teenager like the beginning of another tedious exercise in nostalgia; to those with ears to hear, it is a rich nugget from a lifetime of telling, hearing, and living stories.

The Fall and Rise of Story

One legacy of the Enlightenment and its consequences was the decreased importance of story. Who needs story or myth to make sense of the world when we have the hard sciences? *Story* and *myth* became nearly pejorative terms to describe tales that may have been helpful to premodern, technologically unsophisticated audiences, but not to modern people.

Lately we have sensed that we have become impoverished without story. This sense seems to have taken

24

root with particular intensity in the church. Theologians return to narrative as their preferred method of conceptualizing transcendent reality. Church staffs structure their meetings around telling stories of God changing the lives of individuals in their care. Preachers find that they must hone their storytelling abilities to hold the attention of their congregation.

Story is shaping the face of contemporary evangelism as well. Traditional evangelistic methods in our times have focused on one of two methods: the communication of propositional truth, or an appeal to psychologically based "felt needs." In the first method, the evangelist is concerned with communicating the theological facts of the biblical teaching on salvation, persuading her listener through logical arguments, and calling for acceptance of these facts and a resultant life commitment. In the second instance, the evangelist begins with the needs, desires, and aspirations of the listener, and shapes his presentation of the Christian message accordingly, offering Jesus as the answer to low self-esteem or relational dysfunction. In each case, the "salvation message" is, almost by necessity, atomized and detached from the larger picture of biblical revelation.

Evangelist and author Leighton Ford argues convincingly that effective evangelism in postmodern times will be based on story. It will, in fact, be *narrative* evangelism. Conversion occurs when God's Story calls our stories into question, and we respond. Evangelism takes place when followers of Christ help spiritual seekers see their own stories in the light of God's Story and then embrace this larger Story.[1] Logic and psychological appeal are not discounted completely, but they are subordinated to a big-picture approach to understanding and articulating the Christian message.

25

The Plot Thickens

It is our contention that effective discipleship in post-modern times will be *narrative discipleship*. This is, in effect, the outworking of narrative evangelism. After the stories of our lives are linked with God's Story, the story does not end. Narrative discipleship involves helping followers of Christ see how the unfolding of their own life story is a key part of God's ongoing plot of redemption, as he moves toward the climactic point of history when he will sum up all things in Christ (Eph. 1:10).

When traditional approaches to Christian discipleship focus on the communication of propositional truth, would-be disciples are put through the paces of learning about God and the Christian life. They are armed with a collection of Bible verses to ward off temptation and grow deeper in the faith and they are equipped with sets of spiritual principles designed to help them handle everything from personal finances to having a quiet time to discerning the will of God.

The best of these traditional, or propositional, approaches have recognized the importance of relationship in the discipleship process. To be a discipler is to invest one's life into the life of someone younger in the faith, to encourage them and hold them accountable. But even the relationship-centered approaches to discipleship have emphasized propositional truth and the communication of information. To be a disciple is to grasp and apply a body of information and, in turn, to be able to give this information away.

Much good can be said about this traditional approach. The Navigators, Campus Crusade for Christ, and countless local churches that emphasize propositional discipleship have succeeded in equipping their disciples with essential information for living the Christian life. Schemes for memorizing Bible verses, the routine of a daily quiet time, practical principles for prayer, and other features of propositional discipleship help to create a climate for great spiritual growth and deep understanding of spiritual truth. But we sense among GenXers a yearning for something more than solely information-based discipleship.

A Better Way

The phenomenal popularity of Henry Blackaby's *Experiencing God* material is a clear indicator of this new yearning.[2] Originally conceived as a seminar workbook for use within the Southern Baptist Convention, *Experiencing God* has enjoyed grassroots popularity and launched what nearly amounts to a small industry, encompassing a book, video program, and even a study Bible. In its essence, Blackaby's teaching is that God is at work around us, and we can be involved in his work if we will discover where he is moving and then align our lives to match his purposes.

The wild popularity of the near-narrative approach of *Experiencing God* is an indicator that purely propositional approaches to discipleship are falling short in a culture less and less rooted in a propositional understanding of truth. But even Blackaby's approach is heavy with propositional truth claims and systematic logic. In these postmodern times, it seems clear that a new way is imperative.

An Even Better Way

This new way will involve an increasing reliance on story to foster discipleship. If conversion occurs when our life stories collide with God's Story, then discipleship happens when our ongoing stories are caught up in God's Story, which never ends.

A disciple is one whose life trajectory shows that he is being caught up in a Story larger than his own, as his character is being shaped and transformed to reflect the character of the Storyteller. A disciple lives with reckless hope that, in spite of all appearances and odds, the Story will have a good ending, because the Storyteller is good. And a disciple is convinced in her heart that her life is not a series of random, unconnected events, but that she is a player in the greatest drama of all time, the drama of a lovesick God spurned by his beloved. This is a God who enters into space and time on a cosmic rescue mission to capture hearts and lives and who will one day make all things new. Narrative discipleship is not a battle plan, a job description, or a series of workbooks to be mastered. It is a drama, a life's quest, a Story that is infinitely bigger than any of its characters except for the Hero.

Mixed Blessings

In the modern era, story has faced a credibility problem. When science and empirical investigation are enthroned, myths and stories are little more than interesting diversions or mere fodder for sociological research. At first blush, the postmodern era seems to offer great hope for a narrative approach to evangelism and discipleship. The emphasis on narrative in the social sciences and arts seems to point in this direction. But there is a problem for the Christian story in these postmodern times. The problem involves the Christian claim to moral universality.

Postmodernity is characterized, in its essence, by an aversion to "metanarratives," large scale stories that purport to explain truth and reality for all people of all times and places. Jean-François Lyotard's frequently quoted statement sums up the postmodern posture: "Simplifying in the extreme, I define postmodern as incredulity towards metanarratives."[3]

From a postmodern ethical stance, metanarratives lend themselves all too easily to a belief in absolute truth, which can lead those who believe they possess this truth to marginalize and oppress those outside the pale of the prevailing wisdom, particularly those of other, less powerful, cultures. Because Generation Xers have drunk in postmodernism like mother's milk, it is not difficult to understand the entrenched relativism found in the generation. Truth is seen as a product of a particular time and circumstance, not something objective or universal.

In our experience, this relativism pervades the minds of even many Christian Xers. Young Christians are often quick to acknowledge that Jesus is the only way to God for them but that he may not be for others. By the same token, abortion may be wrong and against God's will *for me,* but not necessarily for my friend.

While metanarratives are suspect, localized, even personalized, narratives are given credibility. It can be argued that one of the key impulses of the multicultural movement is a desire to recognize the legitimacy of the stories and narratives of a wide variety of faith traditions and ethnicities.

While this new openness to the stories of others is encouraging and salutary, the postmodern aversion to metanarratives creates more problems than it solves. The trajectory of history, particularly the very recent history of such countries as Bosnia-Herzegovina, Rwanda, and Burundi, would seem to indicate that localized stories, particularly those revolving around tribal identification and ethnicity, lend themselves to oppression and violence every bit as much as metanarratives.

The end result of the rise of postmodernity has been that the world is now characterized by a loss of trust in stories. "Not only can no story or tradition be regarded as absolute, but postmodern people have come to experience themselves more and more as storyless," write Middleton and Walsh.[4] The title of Robert Jenson's important article in *First Things* sums up the cultural reality: "A World Which Has Lost Its Story."[5]

This ironic new reality of a storyless world that values story holds both promise and peril for the spread of the Christian gospel and the discipleship enterprise with Generation X. We are helped by a new openness to the credibility of the stories of individuals. Christianity is no longer viewed as a priori incredible because it is "antiscientific" or "irrational." The testimony of a life changed by Christ is viewed as relevant. On the other hand, the fact that the Christian faith changes one life is not viewed as meaning that it has relevancy for any other particular life. "Do your own thing" has been elevated from 1960s pseudomorality to 1990s metaphysical truth. Generation X validates individual experience but it is unwilling to concede that individual experience points to normative and universal truth.

The Narrative Moment

Into this cultural moment of great crisis and great opportunity, we enter as would-be disciplers of the first generation raised without religion. Even Christian Xers operate and are influenced by the relativistic milieu of postmodernity. It is clear that traditional, linear methods of propositional discipleship will not be adequate for a new generation. Previous generations of disciplers

30

could hand a disciple a good book, ask him to read the next chapter, and meet for a fruitful discussion. This tends not to work with Generation X because, as one practitioner puts it, "Xers will lose the book!"

We must disciple with narrative, with story. This begins with conversion, when we help Xers understand the big picture of God's Story and how that intersects with their own story. Then we must help a growing Christian see how God's continuing Story, the great plot, is breaking into and shaping his or her own life story. We will help them identify the heartbeat of the great Storyteller and align their own story with his purposes, which involve the coming of a kingdom characterized by faith, hope, and love.

At this point we as disciplers must challenge the GenXer's assumption that metanarratives are invalid. The Christian faith is the great, the true metanarrative. But we will enjoy little success if we challenge this deeply held tenet at the outset. Better to let the plot gain credibility for itself, as the Holy Spirit works to bring sweetness and savor to the Story. We must present the Story with all of the passion and power of which it is worthy. Sweeping images and great romance are not only helpful, but mandatory.

Only a big image will suffice to communicate the Story—an image like a kingdom that is at once glorious and humble, straightforward and subversive, at once as big as all heaven and as small as a tiny mustard seed. Narrative discipleship has as its reference point this mysteriously already–not yet kingdom and its radically countercultural values of faith, hope, and love.

THE STORY
OF THE KINGDOM

Drugs, sex, guns, killing, crime, poetry, style, body piercing, tattoos—it's all part of our culture. But that's not really what worries me. It's the emotion, the ability to feel so much pain, to hate, to love. It's just incredible. Everything seems so big.

Slow Train Coming

The story of the kingdom is the story of God's moving in history to accomplish his purposes. God does not move without regard to people, treating them as pawns in a cosmic chess game or as obstacles standing in his way. Instead, God's purposes are always concerned with people. God is a relational God. He was from the very outset of creation in the garden (Gen. 1) and will be to the culmination of creation in the new city (Rev. 21–22). God's will is worked out in the lives of human beings and, more to the point, human communities. The story

33

of the kingdom is not the story of a far-removed deity exercising his power according to caprice, but rather the story of the subversive, slow-growing realm of faith, hope, and love breaking into the lives of people.

The Old Testament prophets looked forward to the coming of a kingdom in the person of the Messiah. Although the term "kingdom of God" is not found in the Old Testament, shadows of the fuller New Testament–kingdom idea sprinkle its pages. This anticipation is realized most fully in the book of Daniel, where the prophet sees the coming of a kingdom which will crush all other human kingdoms (Daniel 2). In chapter 7 Daniel ties this coming kingdom with the Messianic king (Dan. 7:13–14). Other prophets foresaw the advent of a kingdom characterized by a new covenant rooted in God's forgiveness (Jer. 31:34), the gift of the Holy Spirit (Joel 2:28–29), judgment for those who reject God (Zeph. 1:14–15), healing for those who embrace Messiah (Mal. 4:2), and, significantly, the restoration and re-creation of the cosmos as the new heavens and new earth (Isa. 35; 65:17).

The New Testament brings the kingdom of God from the shadows to center stage. John the Baptizer began his ministry by proclaiming, "Repent, for the kingdom of heaven is near" (Matt. 3:2). It was nearer than his listeners may have thought, for Jesus announced that the kingdom was not only near but, in fact, "at hand" (Mark 1:15 KJV). The thrust of the New Testament is that the kingdom of God was ushered in by Jesus and is tied inextricably to him.

But Delayed at the Station

Biblical scholars have been preoccupied with the topic of the kingdom of God for most of this century.

There is widespread recognition that the kingdom of God was the focal point of Jesus' teaching, but there the agreement ended, at least until recently. One group of scholars argued that the kingdom was an imminent, here-and-now reality brought by Jesus to the world. Others argued that Jesus had in mind a kingdom coming in the future, but not yet present.

The scholarly fascination with the kingdom of God has worked its way down to the popular level, at least in a crude form. A large number of Christians in this century, particularly in North America and the United Kingdom, have viewed the kingdom as a future entity. The dispensational theology, with its cumbersome charts and prophetic schemes, has popularized the idea of the kingdom as part of the prophetic future. Those who hold to this theology tend to be preoccupied with prophetic minutiae and to live with an otherworldly focus. If the promised kingdom is coming somewhere down the pike, after all, why worry about the here and now? Better to watch the newspapers for signs of the end and to huddle together, away from the corrupt world, to preserve purity and holiness.

Other Christians have located the kingdom solely in the present, believing that the kingdom of justice, peace, and mercy promised by Jesus should be a reality right now. This idealism runs headlong into a sin-drenched world, resulting in a determination to make the kingdom come. Inevitably this takes the form of political agitation, whether from the right or left.

Both extremes are, quite simply, wrong. One makes the kingdom a specter for the future, removed from real life. The other centers responsibility for the kingdom's coming in human hands.

More recently there is a growing consensus that the kingdom of God is both present and future, a reality that was ushered in by Jesus but has not yet realized its fullness. This is an important point, one we must not speed past. There are in the Bible clear references to the kingdom as a here-and-now reality (Matt. 12:28; Luke 17:20–21). There are just as clear references to the kingdom as a future entity (Matt. 7:21–23; 2 Tim. 4:18). The fact is that the present–future nature of the kingdom is in balanced tension. And it is this tension that gives the kingdom its romance and intrigue.

Like one of Mozart's melodies, the kingdom is rich and satisfying and very present now; at the same time, the melody causes us to yearn for something else, something we can almost see, but not quite touch. The satisfaction promised is here already. But something inside of us wants more and senses that we are not yet what we were made to be. This is the kingdom of God—already fully present in Jesus at his first coming, but not yet fully realized until Jesus' second coming. In the meantime, we live in this tension between the already and the not yet. The tension makes the kingdom a good story. It is a story that we have all too often missed or squandered.

> . . . the Kingdom of God is the time, or a time beyond time, when it will no longer be humans in their lunacy who are in charge of the world but God in his mercy who will be in charge of the world. It's the time above all else for wild rejoicing—like getting out of jail, like being cured of cancer, like finally, at long last, coming home. And it is at hand, Jesus says.[1]

The invitation given to us in the gospel is the invitation to drop our old allegiances and give ourselves to the new kingdom of God. We are invited to join the new community of others who have found in the already–not yet kingdom their heart's desire, who have recognized the hauntingly beautiful melody playing in the words and life of Jesus. This is the story of the kingdom.

Signs of the Kingdom

To Jesus, the kingdom was never just an abstract concept, dealing with ethereal mysticism, intricate prophetic schemes, or political ideologies. The kingdom relates to organic, flesh and blood life—love, life, death, food, parties, wine. The kingdom has to do with treating your neighbor with kindness, conducting your business with integrity and fairness, caring for the poor and oppressed, having a heart for the marginalized, loving your husband and kids, being willing to be tortured—and even die—for your faith. The values of the kingdom show us how to live in a world that is not fair, among people who will treat us cruelly and casually. More to the point, it helps us understand the extent to which we can be cruel and casual, and how we can be changed. It is a kingdom of countercultural values—faith, hope, and love.

When we disciple, we are introducing new or young Christ-followers to an entirely new way of living, to this new value system. As we have seen, Xers live in a world where faith is subjective, valuable only to the individual, and shouldn't interfere with anyone else's worldview or impinge on what one wants. Hope is something that applies at best to one's own life, certainly not the world at large, which is already shot to pieces. Love is an overused word peddled by advertisers to a generation that has been loved little and knows how to love less. "I love you, man," which could have been the cry of a stoned hippie in the '60s or a "sensitive male" in the '70s is in the '90s the deeply cynical line of a shiftless guy who wants nothing more than a Bud Light. Love is something you say to get what you want, reasons a cynical generation. But faith, hope, and love are the leading qualities of life in the kingdom and form the matrix of narrative discipling.

If narrative discipling begins when we help Xers see that their stories have collided with God's Story and they choose to become part of the larger Story, then it begins to take form and shape when we introduce them to the plot themes of faith, hope, and love. Faith is rooted in the present nature of the kingdom—the life, death, and resurrection of Christ in real time. Hope looks forward to the future aspect of the kingdom—Christ's return and the new heavens and new earth. And love is an outgrowth of a life taken up with faith and hope.

Faith, hope, and love are the values of the kingdom for all generations and all times. But the multifaceted nature of the kingdom means that some of its characteristics will have particular resonance at certain times. We believe that four qualities of life in the kingdom speak with urgency to Generation X: relationships in community, forgiveness, suffering, and reconciliation.

Relationships in Community

In *Reckless Hope* we argued at length that community is part of the essence of the gospel. Generation X highly values relational interconnectedness, yet many members of the generation seem not to know how to relate. The gospel calls us from our shattered relationships, estrangement, isolation, and abuse-filled backgrounds to the new, safe community of God's people, who have experienced Christ's graciously liberating love. The community is not utopian, because it is made up of sinful people, but it is at its best a taste of life in the already, the way it will be finally in the not yet.

The Bible speaks very little of "me and Jesus." It speaks a lot about "us and Jesus." Counter to North American individualism, life in the kingdom is made up of interdependent people. One of the first elements of narrative discipleship is helping Xers to see that they are now part of a wider community. The kingdom of God is much bigger than the church, the new community, but this community is the most important product of the kingdom. While the idea of giving oneself to a community is attractive to Xers, it will still be a difficult adjustment. We have been burned in relationships and by institutions, which means that we are slow to join or commit. We are deeply cynical, which means that we find it difficult to trust others, particularly people we don't know very well.

So the narrative discipler must do two main things. First, he must pour his life into his friend. Narrative discipleship is intensely personal. The narrative discipler is a part of the Story with the disciple, as a friend and fellow learner. Narrative discipleship will take much longer than conventional propositional discipleship, because most Xers have less of the content background of the faith and because they need more relational development.

Second, the narrative discipler constantly shows his friend how he is part of a bigger Story than the smaller story of his life and the lives of a few friends. This is hard but important work.

Forgiveness

Although the Old Testament understanding of the kingdom was shadowy, one element was crystal clear: The kingdom would be marked by forgiveness of sins (Jer. 31:34; Isa. 33:24). One of the signs that the kingdom had broken into history in the person of Jesus was the fact that he forgave sins scandalously.

Life in the kingdom today will be marked by forgiveness. Past generations, living in a culture that still emphasized personal responsibility, had a sense of personal wrongdoing. Two generations ago, the appeal to have one's sins washed away struck a responsive chord. Today, in a culture marked by blame-shifting and a victim mentality, such an appeal meets some resistance. Deep down, however, we do understand that we are sinners in need of forgiveness, especially when we catch a glimpse of God's holiness and perfection. Generation X is not idealistic about the human condition. The promise of forgiveness still strikes at the human heart, particularly for a generation that has seen so much evil so early in life.

Forgiveness has a particular resonance for Xers, however, when they are challenged to forgive others. Many Xers will have to work through forgiving parents who abandoned or abused them. They will have to forgive political and cultural leaders who failed them. They will need to forgive a government that seems destined to hand them a backbreaking national debt. And they will have to forgive the Baby Boomers, who all too often failed to practice what they preached so loudly. The fact that many Xers have lived such tumultuous lives implies that there is a lot of forgiving to do. They must first see themselves in need of forgiveness, accept that forgiveness, and then learn to forgive others from the heart. A skilled narrative discipler will probe an Xer's story, bringing to light dark places of bitterness, abuse, and hurt, and gently press for healing forgiveness.

Suffering

It is axiomatic that Christians in the First World know little about suffering, at least compared to our Third World brethren, as well as much of the Christian community throughout history. This may be changing. Xers have seen more and experienced more by the end of their junior high years than their forebears had by middle age. Gangs, violence, AIDS, and the prevalence of sexual abuse have caused Xers to grow up before their time.

The gospel makes sense of suffering, particularly to a generation for which suffering is real, not just an apologetic challenge. While we may not be able to offer definitive answers for the problem of evil or why children are abused, we can offer a God who knows suffering personally. "Christianity's image is singular and earthly: God on the cross, his arms splayed outward, his eyes wide open in agony. He is a God with a face. He is Jesus."[2]

Skewed formulations of the gospel such as "health and wealth" or "the victorious Christian life" fall on deaf ears in Generation X. Our generation wants and needs a gospel that addresses the human condition with both truth and hope and that allows room for the mystery of suffering. Narrative disciplers have the difficult joy of helping their friends face up to the reality of suffering and to help them find meaning for this suffering in the person of Jesus. Perhaps more than previous generations, Generation X may be able to reflect Christ's compassion for those who suffer, the kind of compassion that comes only from a life acquainted personally with sorrow and grief.

Reconciliation

The message of reconciliation permeates the Bible. God is concerned with reconciling people to himself, with reconciling people to people, and with reconciling people to the created order. In fact reconciliation is a near obsession with God, who "does not take away life; instead, he devises ways so that a banished person may not remain estranged from him" (2 Sam. 14:14). The message of the gospel is that God has reconciled men and women to himself through Christ. The implication of this is that we have been entrusted now with speaking this message of reconciliation to others and are, in fact, agents and ambassadors of reconciliation (2 Cor. 5:18–19). Furthermore, reconciliation has cosmic dimensions as well. Ephesians 1 and Colossians 1 indicate that our reconciliation to God is bound up with the reconciliation of the whole created order, which groans now with painful anticipation as it waits for the ultimate reconciliation of God and mankind (Rom. 8:19–22). God is interested in mending broken relationships and putting things right.

Perhaps no other aspect of life in the kingdom resonates with Xers like this one. Our generation is painfully aware that something is wrong with its relationships, that we are broken people who need to be fixed. We are committed to racial reconciliation like no generation before. We long for our families of origin to be put together, for our own families, if we can find the courage to form them, to stay together. But we don't dare to hope.

Can it be true that things can last, that I can love over time, that someone can care for me and not, at last, go away? I want to believe this but I almost don't allow myself. An Xer sat recently in one of our offices, wrestling with the message of the reconciling gospel. His face was creased with emotion, his fists were clenched, almost as if he were in pain. "I really want to believe this stuff," he said, "but I don't think I can. It seems too good to be true that somebody did that for me and all I have to do is accept it and link up with Jesus' people. Nothing has ever sounded that good before. But I've tried other stuff, and people and things always let me down. No one keeps their promises in the

42

end. Why should Jesus be any different? I mean, I want to believe that he is, but how can I?"

He left the office still clinging to his doubts. And his question haunts. He, and millions like him, need to believe that someone will come through for them, that someone will keep his promises. "Believe in me. Help me believe in anything. I want to be someone who believes."[3] He doesn't need to hear promises or a party line; he needs to hear and rehear a story about a Man who kept all his promises and who formed a community of people who try and sometimes fail to keep their promises but who never quit trying. He needs to hear a story about a kingdom that is bigger than he, bigger than anything, but that he can enter anytime he wants and join forever as a son, brother, and friend.

"The Kingdom of God is where we belong," writes Frederick Buechner. "It is home, and whether we realize it or not, I think we are all of us homesick for it."[4] He is exactly right.

WHEN STORIES COLLIDE

It's hard . . . hard . . . hard to see any sort of optimism, any sort of order in the future when I can't take care of simple things like school, family, work, responsibilities, and relationships—the most standard parts of life there are. It's incredible how the simplest things, the most common things, can be hard if not nearly impossible to balance.

A Changed Heart

Ian's experience of God was the same as his experience of his father. God was angry, tyrannical, never to be pleased—just like his dad. Ian spent his whole life trying to please his father but could never do it. He has a distinct memory of crying his eyes out in sixth grade. He had gotten a 95 on a spelling test and his father grounded him for a week. He said, "You knew all of those words; you should have gotten a 100."

In college he struggled through his business classes because his dad told him he needed to get a business degree. During his sophomore year, he wanted to change

45

his major to history, one subject for which he had some true passion. He called home to get his father's opinion—and approval. On the phone his idea was met by an icy silence followed by a curt, "It's your life. You can screw it up if you want to."

So he graduated with a business degree and took a job that made him miserable. His dad never said he was proud. He only asked, "How much are they paying you these days?" Ian felt a knot in his stomach every time he heard that question.

He couldn't maintain a relationship with a woman either. He always found himself feeling jealous and needing to control her. He could be demeaning and manipulative. It sounded familiar—like a relationship he had observed for more than twenty years.

At twenty-four Ian was despondent. He hated his job; he hated himself; he hated his life. He believed in God but only because he feared not believing in him. God was a scary, angry man waiting to find his failings. In the accounts of Jesus' life and ministry, Ian never saw love and compassion. He saw only anger. "Didn't Jesus turn over the tables in the temple? And he yelled at the Pharisees," he observed. "He seemed to hate his disciples too," he said. "He was always complaining about them. He said they never had enough faith or didn't follow directions or whatever."

Ian's rage was almost palpable. He suffered from his father's disastrous legacy almost down to his core. When he entered into a discipling relationship with an elder from his church, it was because he needed the approval of an older man, not because he wanted to know God better. He was full of self-hatred and already bitter at an early age. He needed help.

A year later Ian is a different man. You don't feel tension when you talk to him. You notice he has a sharp sense of humor and his self-deprecating jokes are born out of humility and not self-loathing. He has a few close friends. He's not dating anyone and probably won't for a while but he's growing in his understanding of how to treat women. More important, his relationship with God is much better. He has allowed God to be all that he has revealed himself to be, not just a two-dimensional caricature. Yes, God is still angry at times but God is also loving and gracious and merciful and even kind.

Two things are clear about what happened. First, it is clear that God did it. God's Holy Spirit made a change in this young man. Second, it is also clear that God used the relationship with an older man as a vehicle of change. When this wise man talks about what happened—and *is* happening—in their relationship, he doesn't give you a great formula. It isn't a matter of reading the right book or memorizing the right verses or learning the right gospel outline, though these are all worthy and important activities. Instead, something more subtle and powerful is involved.

The truth is that Ian changed because this man related to him the way Jesus would. He modeled himself after Jesus and found that right balance of compassion and truth, of tenderness and toughness, of sacrificial acts and radical resistance. The power of discipling relationships is this: *People change when we relate to them the way Jesus would.*

How Jesus Treated People

Jesus Always Told the Truth

None of us can ever relate to people exactly the way Jesus did. We are most imperfect much of the time. However, we are called to be imitators of Christ, and this certainly applies to how we conduct ourselves in relationships. There are some clear understandings of Jesus' style of relating that apply to the context of discipling.

First, we know that Jesus always spoke truth. He told the truth about himself, about his Father, about others, about the condition of the world. Jesus' every utterance was truthful. He did not soft-pedal or flatter. His words had integrity, and people could count on what he said. Truth permeated all of his interactions. Sometimes the truth hurt; sometimes it soothed.

The application to discipling is clear. We are called to relate the way Jesus would by being truthful in what we say. Imitating Jesus in our discipling relationships means being a truth-teller. We speak the truth to spur our disciples on to action or cause them to turn away from behaviors that dishonor God. We also speak it to comfort people when they are hurting or doubting.

We want to be encouraging but we should encourage only with words of truth. Flattery helps no one. It gives the disciple inaccurate feedback and it undermines the credibility of the mentor.

Some Christians make the opposite mistake, however, believing that telling the truth is a license to be harsh and critical. It is not. Telling the truth well means considering the needs of others. It involves choosing words that best motivate people toward godliness. Discipling relationships should be based on speaking words of truth to each other.

Jesus Saw the Potential in Others

Peter was fishing when Jesus first called him. Peter dropped his net and never looked back. All of his life Peter had been impulsive. Even after Jesus called him, he was hotheaded and impetuous, blurting out the wrong responses. Once Jesus had to say to him, "Get behind me, Satan! You are a stumbling block to me" (Matt. 16:23).

Peter constantly ran his mouth without thinking. The transfiguration of Jesus on the mountaintop was glorious and spectacular. There was Jesus, along with Moses and Elijah, glowing white. In the middle of this amazing event, Peter couldn't be quiet and respect the holiness of the moment; he blurted out something inane. The Gospel writer says that Peter "did not know what he was saying" (Luke 9:33). Peter often didn't know what he was saying.

On one occasion Jesus wanted to teach his disciples an important lesson. By washing their feet, he would communicate their need to be cleansed by him, while at the same time modeling servant-leadership. Peter was appalled at the sight of his master kneeling to wash dirty feet and Peter refused to let him do it. After Jesus explained his intent, Peter blurted out, "not just my feet but my hands and my head as well!" (John 13:9). Peter often missed the point.

Before Jesus was arrested and crucified, Peter loudly announced that he would rather die than deny Christ. When the soldiers came to get Jesus, Peter lunged forward with his sword and cut off the right ear of the high priest's servant. You can hear the frustration in Jesus' voice when he commands, "Put your sword away!" (John 18:10–11). Peter often acted on impulse.

As you recall, Peter did deny Christ three times that night—even once to a little girl. He doesn't sound like the model disciple. Yet Jesus saw great potential in him. In the middle of it all, Jesus said to him, "And I tell you that you are Peter, and on this rock I will build my church, and the gates of Hades will not overcome it. I will give you the keys of the kingdom of heaven; whatever you bind on earth will be bound in heaven, and whatever you loose on earth will be loosed in heaven" (Matt. 16:18–19).

The amazing part of the story was that Peter did become the rock. We see a different Peter in the book of Acts than the man in the Gospels. We see a Peter who is eloquent, reflective, and bold. He became a new man because of what Jesus did in his life.

Jesus saw the potential in the impetuous Peter. He looked at this diamond in the rough and saw the man Peter could and would become. For us the implications are clear. Looking out for the obviously gifted potential disciple is also legitimate. (Jesus did this, too.) But we should not rule out investing ourselves in young men and women with rough edges.

Ian's story is not even halfway finished, but it's clear that he is already a better man because someone invested in him. He would not likely have made anyone's A-list of potential disciples, but someone who trusted God saw the potential in him.

A word of caution: Discipling is not therapy. The admonition here is not to seek out disciples just because they are needy or emotionally damaged and try to fix them. Rather, our charge is to see the potential in young men and women, from the shining all-stars to the unpolished benchwarmers. We move faithfully into the life of whomever God has brought into our life.

Jesus Responded Uniquely to Individuals

The Gospel accounts are full of stories illustrating the compassion of Jesus. One beautiful sequence in the Gospel of Mark shows Jesus calming a raging storm to comfort his terrified disciples, liberating a man whose life had been destroyed by a legion of demons, healing a chronically ill woman, and bringing a dead girl back to life (see Mark 4:35–5:43). In doing so, he not only demonstrated his authority over sickness, death, the natural, and the supernatural, but he also showed deep compassion for others. Matthew writes in his Gospel, "When he saw the crowds, he had compassion on them, because they were harassed and helpless, like sheep without a shepherd" (Matt. 9:36).

Jesus also raged against the religious leaders of the day, calling them hypocrites, blind fools, snakes, and whitewashed tombs. He flipped the tables over in the temple. He often said strong words to people.

Jesus interacted differently with people to meet unique needs. His words and actions perfectly suited each individual and each situation. Jesus knew who needed to be comforted and who needed to be riled. He knew who needed a gentle touch and who needed to be shaken.

He also changed his teaching style to best fit the individual and the situation. In many instances he spoke in parables to groups. In doing so, some people missed the point, but those who were spiritually hungry ate it up. At other times he taught directly and with specific instruction. Sometimes he used hyperbole to make his point, while being extremely concrete and exact on other occasions.

The implications are clear for disciplers. Cookie-cutter approaches to disciple making should be discarded. Some churches and other ministries have extraordinarily rigid programs for discipling. Each disciple reads the same book, memorizes the same verses, attends the same trainings, and so on. Uniformity does accomplish a certain degree of quality control—and some of these programs have excellent content—but it does not allow us to respond uniquely to people the way Jesus did.

We can disciple individually or in groups but we would always be wise to use a flexible array of approaches, depending on what the person or group needs to grow in their faith. All of our stories connect with the same larger Story that God is telling, but each of us is living a unique part of it. Two twenty-four-year-olds from the same church may be similar in many ways, but each is in the early chapters of her own story. Each has different gifts, different needs, and a different calling. God has made them different on purpose. They each have a unique story to tell and to live.

Jesus Showed Grace

Jesus was having dinner at the home of a Pharisee when a woman with a bad reputation slipped inside to see him. She was so overcome with grief—presumably over her own sinfulness—that her tears began to drip onto his feet. She knelt down, mopped his feet with her own hair, kissed them, and poured perfume on them. The Pharisee sniffed in contempt. *If this man were really a prophet, he would know what kind of dreadful woman this is,* he thought. Jesus knew the man's thoughts and proceeded to tell the woman that her sins were forgiven. "Your faith has saved you," he said to her. Even though she was filthy from sin, her repentance and faith had made her clean. She cleansed his feet; he cleansed her soul (see Luke 7:36–50).

She was saved by the grace of God. Over and over again Jesus demonstrated grace to others. He showed grace in the way that he responded and by the things he taught. The good news of the Bible is that we are saved by grace through faith in Jesus. It is in that grace that we also live. We don't try to convince ourselves that we can be good enough to earn salvation. Predictably, when we live under grace, we are actually more motivated to live in a way that honors God. When we see how dearly

God loves us, we are compelled to demonstrate our love for him.

Despite this reality, we have a nasty habit of trying to put people back under the law. We have our spiritual checklists that we use as gauges of maturity and orthodoxy. In discipling relationships we often have standards of thought and behavior that we use to assess our disciple's level of commitment to the Lord. Often these standards look the same for each disciple.

In many instances Scripture is seen as a tool for making behavior conform to certain specifications. Like Jesus, we should show those we disciple what it means to experience grace. If they mess up, we don't become a punishing authority figure. ~~We never excuse or minimize sin but we show grace.~~

There is always a tricky balancing act when it comes to being a person who lives under grace. Paul wrestled with this balance in the Book of Romans. You are saved by grace, he writes. You have freedom in Christ. Please don't use that freedom to do anything you want. Use it to honor God. For pages and pages he builds his argument. He takes such pains, though, to let us know that we really are not under the law any more. We are to live in the grace of God (Romans 5–6). For some reason, though, something in us makes us want to crawl back under the heavy hand of the law. In doing so, we often place this same burden on others.

Putting people under the law can change behavior. It gets outward results. Unfortunately it does not change hearts. It does not allow people to be captured by grace, to weep over sin because it breaks the heart of God. ~~When we show grace to those we disciple, we let people fall in love with God in new and fresh ways. In doing so, their hearts become tender toward God again. It becomes their desire to honor God with their whole life.~~

People change when we relate to them the way Jesus would. This means we tell the truth in our relationships. It means we see the potential in others. It means we respond to each individual uniquely. It means we show them grace and don't put them under the law. When we do these things, God moves and people change.

When Stories Collide

There have been many philosophies developed around how potential disciples should be chosen. Some churches and parachurches emphasize looking out for the faithful, available, and teachable—or FAT—people to disciple. Others focus on those who appear to be leadership material. Some others lean in the opposite direction and advise pursuing those who don't seem to fit in or who might not thrive spiritually without a mentor.

All of these philosophies make sense but they each miss an obvious point: God causes our lives to intersect the lives of certain other people. When these people happen to be younger in their faith, they are often the ones God would have us disciple, whether they are leaders, wallflowers, or in between.

Consider how Jesus picked his disciples. He was walking beside the Sea of Galilee and he saw two brothers, Peter and Andrew, both fishermen. He said, "Follow me," and they dropped their nets and followed him. Then he saw two other brothers fishing. They were in their boat and he said, "Follow me," and they hopped out of the boat and followed him. Then he saw Matthew sitting in the tax collector's booth and he said, "Follow me," and Matthew jumped out of the booth and followed him. The men Jesus chose as his disciples were those he ran across in his daily life.

If God is in control and we are living faithfully, then we will quite naturally intersect the lives of others who need to be discipled. God has given each of us unique gifts and interests. If we are all doing our part, we will cover the range of individuals. For example, a person with a gift of mercy may be naturally drawn to those who do not fit in well. An evangelist may gravitate toward those whom he has led to Christ. An exhorter may move toward someone who is not realizing her potential. Or we may just disciple those whom God has caused us to bump into. Our stories collide.

God is telling a story through each of us. He is at work knitting together our smaller stories into the larger Story that he is telling. When an older believer becomes involved in the life of a younger believer, their stories collide and deep change can occur. As disciplers, we allow ourselves to be changed and shaped by the relationship. We sense our own story being expanded and textured as we help mold the story of the younger brother or sister. The young disciple is not the only one who should be changed by the relationship. We should be changed as well.

We Still Thirst

We return to the woman at the well. Jesus teaches her about this living water. One taste and you will never thirst again. She is interested. How does she get this water?

"Go get your husband," he says.

"I don't have a husband," she replies, feigning innocence.

"I know," he says gently, "you have had *five* husbands—and you aren't married to the man you are living with now."

55

Perhaps she blushes. The conversation continues a little longer before she runs excitedly back to town.

"Everybody! Come see this man who told me everything I ever did! Could this be the Messiah?"

The residents run out to meet him. Many Samaritans become believers that day because of a woman who was changed by Jesus (see John 4:1–30).

The gospel comes alive here. Jesus tells her he's got good news: living water. He whets her thirst to know more but before he tells her what this living water is all about, he exposes the worst part of her. She has a secret that she prefers to keep from him. She has a long string of failed relationships and an immoral lifestyle. She doesn't exactly lie to Jesus; she just hides the facts.

Notice that he exposes her not to condemn, but to heighten her thirst for God. Her response to his uncovering words seems tangential at first. She begins by saying that he must be some kind of prophet and then rambles on about where Jews and Samaritans are supposed to worship.

If you consider that this is a woman who has just been exposed, her words make sense. Perhaps you have had a conversation with a nonbeliever who was experiencing shame or crisis and was sharing his struggle with you. If he knew you to be a Christian, he may have blurted out awkwardly that he needs to go back to church or start praying again or something . . . religious.

There is something about being exposed—as vulnerable or foolish or grotesque—that heightens our thirst for God. That was what the woman was doing. Her reply makes perfect sense: They were the unpolished words of a woman who knew she needed Jesus.

Jesus met her that day. He spoke words of hard truth to her. But he saw the potential in her even when others in his culture viewed her as lower-class and immoral. He responded to her in a unique way. He drew her into the conversation with a topic that grabbed her attention—living water. Once he saw her spiritual thirst, he spoke to her plainly about who he was. And she believed.

Jesus showed grace to this thirsty woman. She would have been easy to condemn, to put under the law. Instead, Jesus showed her grace and she changed. She changed for eternity. We can help people change too when we relate to them the way Jesus would.

An Altar to an Unknown God

All I see are people hurting. There's sadness everywhere. What'll make people see Jesus? Why does it have to be that people are OK with living a mediocre life? I don't know what to tell them.

Christians and Culture

The host of a radio call-in show is debating an increasingly frustrated caller. Finally the caller blurts out, "You might try going to church sometime! Then maybe you wouldn't have so many crazy, liberal ideas!" He slams down the phone. The caller, who had earlier revealed himself to be a Christian, represents the frustrations of many believers today in dealing with the culture. They reason that the culture is bad, full of anti-Christian ideas, and therefore must be forcefully opposed.

Christian opposition to the culture is often quite harsh and even coercive at times. It takes many forms, from boycotts to letters to the editor. While some believe we are fighting for righteousness, there is the danger that we may have instead become just another easily offended special-interest group.

Helping GenXers grow up in their faith should include teaching them how a Christian thinks about and engages the culture. Narrative discipling sees the culture as the dangerous setting for a spectacular story. We do not attack the inhabitants of the culture; we rescue them. We act shrewdly, not for self-protection, but to bring others into the kingdom.

Lessons from *The Lion King*

As remarkable as it may seem, *The Lion King* became a giant Rorschach test in which nearly every special-interest group in the country saw its own devils. The 1994 animated Disney feature appears benign enough on the surface. It is about a young lion's coming of age following the death of his father. In classic Disney style it is full of bad guys and comic sidekicks. Who would have guessed that beneath its facade there was a multitude of threatening, hateful messages?

To the feminists *The Lion King* was an offense because the men were the rulers—the king and his heir—and the women were subjugated to them. The lionesses were mere mothers and caretakers while the men had the positions of power. To the homosexuals the slightly effeminate villainous lion was a clear attempt to associate homosexuals with evil conspirators. To various ethnic groups the villain's henchmen represented efforts to suggest that they were aggressive predators because the characters were voiced by ethnic actors.

And what about Christians? We saw a full frontal assault on Christian beliefs and traditional values. We saw monkeys practicing spiritism and witchcraft. We saw occult activity, like summoning the spirits of the dead. We even saw the word S-E-X written in the stars. At least some of us did.

Some Christians began to organize boycotts against Disney movies and theme parks. A few Christian publications blasted Disney. One publicized report even had Christians referring to Disney management as "pedophiles" and "perverts."

The reaction to these histrionics was predictable and, in fact, warranted. A Disney spokesman said plainly, "This is silly." Others were less kind. One letter to the editor in *Entertainment Weekly* was sharp with sarcasm: "Silly me, I thought [Christians] were tending to the poor or finding homes for unwanted children. Who knew they were studying movies like . . . *The Lion King* to save us from subversive messages!"

The same phenomenon unfolded again the following year with *Pocahontas,* which managed to inflame feminists, Native Americans, historians, and of course Christians, who bashed it for its presentation of "ecological spiritism." (The film's senior animator was Glen Keane, a Christian who has kept a daily prayer journal for twenty years and who has Colossians 3:23 on his drawing board: "Whatever you do, work at it with all your heart, as working for the Lord, not for men.")

One could argue that Disney suddenly began making offensive films in the '90s or, more convincingly, that these reactions tell us much about the ways in which our culture has changed. Can you imagine what the response would have been if a film like *Snow White* had been made in the '90s? It's about a woman who cohabits with seven men! This sexist film shows the woman doing housework while the men go off to work. The men, all of whom are dwarves, are given demeaning names like Dopey and Grumpy. The woman's evil stepmother

61

uses her occult powers to consult a magic mirror for information about the future. It would have been a field day.

The point is that Disney hasn't changed as much as we have. As our postmodern culture becomes increasingly fragmented, cause groups begin clamoring for their "rights" and viciously attacking those who may interfere with them. They fight back at any perceived affront; any disagreement is labeled an "outrage." Their sense of humor goes out the window as they view themselves and their cause with deadly seriousness. The notion of working for the collective good disintegrates into a brawl.

Christians join in, using warfare language and mounting up for battle. We battle the culture, decrying everything from Power Rangers to Barney the Dinosaur to news broadcasts. We rage at public educators and artists and homosexuals and feminists and liberals—and the list goes on.

On the surface we appear to be concerned with promoting godliness. However, a sharper analysis suggests that these skirmishes are more often motivated by fear. We are fearful that as Christians we are losing our place at the head of the table as the dominant molders and shapers of the culture's mindset. This is a scary, unsettling prospect for many people. John Woodbridge writes, "We may bemoan a moral decline in the country. Our actual concern, if the truth be known, is not to see a vital Christianity flourish, but rather to secure a more orderly and less violent society in which to live out comfortable and self-satisfied lives."[1]

In a well-publicized news story, a circuit court judge posted the Ten Commandments in his courtroom and invited pastors in to pray over the juries. He is quoted as saying, "If we don't take a stand, it won't be long until the church and the people of God will be persecuted."

A scriptural view of the Church shows us *likely* to endure persecution, rejection, and hostility. In our culture, we were comfortable with being the leaders of the consensus worldview. This is no longer true and it frightens us. In response we have lashed out. We have fought and adopted the language of war. The problem is that we have savaged the very ones that desperately need the gospel. We have demonized them and turned them into our enemies.

People who are not believers *should* be expected to view Christian ideas as bigoted and crazy. As foreign as it seems to most of us, the gospel and the Christian faith are—and *should be*—an outrage to people. Those who do not know God and who are not filled with his Holy Spirit *should* view a Christian's way of thinking as highly offensive, even dangerous. Paul wrote, "The sinful mind is hostile to God. It does not submit to God's law, *nor can it do so*" (Rom. 8:7, emphasis added). How easily we forget that nonbelievers are casualties of the true war—a spiritual war—and have been blinded by the evil one. They are doing what seems right to them. They are thinking as we would think, if it were not for the grace of God.

Jesus said, "Love your enemies and pray for those who persecute you" (Matt. 5:44). This is a far cry from the way we sometimes live. We get so caught up in our fearfulness that we end up hating instead of loving. The charge of the narrative discipler is to help Xers think differently about our culture and the nonbelievers who populate it.

The Culture as Milieu for the Story

According to novelist Orson Scott Card, there are four elements to any story: idea, events, character, and milieu.[2] The *idea* is the information that we are to learn or discover as the story unfolds. The *events* of the story refer to all the action that occurs. The *character* is the nature of the actors in the story, including what motivates their behavior. And *milieu* is the world around the characters in which the events unfold and the ideas are learned.

In God's Story, the *idea* to be learned is that mankind has rebelled against him, has gotten lost, and now needs to be rescued. These renegades think they can make life work better on their own. Instead, they have found themselves lost, confused, and trapped. Worse yet, most of them have no sense that their plight is desperately bleak. They forge ahead, unaware that they are headed for certain doom. How will God rescue his people, even when they do not realize they are in danger?—a great set-up for a wonderful Story. That is the idea.

The *events* of the Story involve great, heroic action. God sends his Son down on a rescue mission. The Son knows that he must die at the end of the mission to save the renegades. By dying, he pays the price that is demanded for them, and then they are free to return to their Father. In a surprise ending, the Son returns to life in a dazzling demonstration of his power over death. Still, some of the renegades come back; some don't. The Son sends out more and more of his followers on rescue missions to finish the job.

The *characters* of this Story are the Father, his Son, their followers, and the renegades. There is also an evil one in the Story, a villain. He and his followers lure the rebels into traps and try to block their return to the Father.

Finally, the *milieu* of this Story is the world around the characters. It is the culture that surrounds the rebels and followers. Both the Father and the Evil One have invaded and marked the milieu. Both followers and

64

renegades have influenced it. The followers of the Father see the milieu as the setting for the rescue mission. It is a place to be shrewdly invaded, snatching up renegades and returning them to live with the Father.

This understanding shapes our view of the culture. It is the setting for a Story that God is telling. Lately we have forgotten the idea of the Story. We remember a few scenes—the ones that involve warfare and conflict—but we do not remember the heart of it. It is a rescue mission born out of love.

Because we have forgotten this, we engage in battle, attacking the ones we were sent to liberate. We try to take back lost territory; we fight for "our" land and "our" country. We see the culture as land to be gained or repossessed in battle, not a backdrop for a spectacular rescue.

We can recapture the sense that these renegades among us are blinded by the evil one, unable to make their way back home, often unaware that they are in danger. They are not to be thrashed, but redeemed. In this great and courageous act of rescue, we can use the culture wisely to help us in our mission.

Using the Words of the Culture

When Paul the apostle was in Athens, he found himself in a culture that was dominated by many competing philosophies and religions. The factual account of his visit says that he was "distressed" by all of the idols that he saw. His ideas were ridiculed by those who held that pleasure was the primary goal of life, as well as by those who claimed reason was the key to fulfillment.

Instead of denouncing them, Paul looked for an opportunity to talk about Jesus. Previously, when he had spoken to Jewish audiences, he connected Jesus the

Messiah to Jewish history. That approach would obviously not go over well with this crowd of Greek intellectuals. He chose another tactic. He picked something from the culture that distressed him and used it shrewdly. He stood up on a hill, surrounded by the Greeks and said, "Men of Athens! I see that in every way you are very religious. For as I walked around and looked carefully at your objects of worship, I even found an altar with this inscription: TO AN UNKNOWN GOD. Now what you worship as something unknown I am going to proclaim to you" (Acts 17:22–23). Paul took the very thing that distressed him and used it to advance God's Story. He was not reactionary. He did not protest or boycott. Instead, he saw opportunity to tell the Story.

He goes on to build an argument that will direct many of them to the true God. When he wants to make a point about God the Creator's relationship to us, Paul quotes someone from their culture. He says, "*As some of your own poets have said,* 'We are his offspring'" (Acts 17:28, emphasis added). He used the words of the culture to speak back to the culture. He quoted their own poets to bolster his argument.

Imagine what would happen if we taught a generation of young believers how to think like Paul. Instead of distancing ourselves from the culture or lashing out at it, we could teach them how to think critically about what they were seeing and to use it shrewdly.

For example, consider the song "One of Us," a former top-ten hit. It was written by Eric Bazilian and sung by Joan Osborne, neither of whom are Christians. The song asks the questions, "What if God were one of us? Just a slob like one of us? Just a stranger on the bus, trying to make his way home?" In this current climate of attack, some believers might focus on the implication that God could be a "slob" and miss an extraordinary opportunity. God is not a slob, we could respond, but He *was* one of us. To a generation that does not know Jesus, this could be a thrilling opportunity to hear about God's Story.

While the Joan Osborne song is an obvious example of how we could use the words of the culture to pique interest in Jesus, there are dozens of examples every year that often slip past us. Movies, TV shows, books, magazines, and other forms of media have opportunities tucked in them. Go back to our original example of *The Lion King.* If we were not so reactive, we could have seen many possibilities to engage the culture with the Story. After all, isn't it also about a kingdom with a king's son for a hero?

Another Disney film maligned by Christians, *The Little Mermaid,* also depicts a kingdom. It portrays one of the most striking metaphors for how God rescued us. The king's daughter becomes ensnared by the evil one because of her own selfishness. To release her, the king has to give himself up for her. He literally sacrifices himself and his position to free her.

Some examples are less safe. *Schindler's List* shows us the evil within the human heart in harrowing detail. It is a graphic depiction of Jeremiah 17:9: "The heart is deceitful above all things and beyond cure. Who can understand it?" But the film also powerfully teaches us what it means to be redeemed.

There are other, innumerable examples in all forms of media. We can reframe our thinking about the culture by exposing ourselves to the media with the purpose of looking for themes that may provide opportunities to tell the story. Instead of being on the attack, we can use the words and images in a way that can further the spreading of God's Story.

There are times, though, when speaking harsh words to the culture is necessary and appropriate. Paul found himself in this situation as well and he used the same tactic; he let the culture speak for itself. He was writing to Titus, a Greek believer whom he had personally taught and discipled. Titus had become overseer of the churches on the island of Crete but was running into some difficulty with a contingent of "rebellious people." Paul uses the words of the culture in his rebuke. He writes, "Even one of their own prophets has said, 'Cretans are always liars, evil brutes, lazy gluttons.' This testimony is true" (Titus 1:12–13). This was a line from a poem by Epimenides, an early resident of Crete. Essentially Paul is saying, "Titus, what the culture says about itself confirms your frustrations."

When we need to speak strong words, we can let the culture speak for itself. The culture says much about the damage done by broken promises, the emotional consequences of premarital sex, the subtle horrors of selfishness, and the general condition of mankind. Hold up lyrics and script lines and visual images as mirrors to the culture, saying, "This is what we are like. This is why we need God."

When a TV character talks of the "empty place" in her heart, when a rock vocalist sings of a "world of lies," or when the murderer in a novel says he feels "human, exactly like everyone else," we have the culture speaking harsh truth to itself. Our challenge is to reflect these messages back to the culture and then offer hope—the hope found in the Story of a lovesick God who longs for the return of his children.

6
Eyes, Ears, and Stinky Feet

God's purpose: I don't have a clue what it is. But Dave definitely seems to think it has something to do with evangelism. I really do enjoy telling people about my experience.

What We Bring to the Table

Potlucks have become a regular part of our community times. Everyone brings something. One night almost everyone brought dessert. On another night it was all main courses—no side dishes, no drinks. We have gotten out of balance on occasion, but for the most part it all seems to work together. In a sense, these potlucks are a metaphor for how well we function as a group. Sometimes we get out of balance in our relationships and responsibilities but generally speaking we work well together.

As with the potlucks we each have something special to contribute to the community. It may be a flashy main

69

dish; it may be a side dish or dessert—or it may even be cups and napkins. But we each bring something important and unique to it.

In the Bible Paul used a different metaphor for how we should function as a community of believers. He said it's as if we are all different parts that come together to form a whole body. The parts are all interdependent and each one is important for the body to function well. You need eyes to see, ears to hear, feet to walk. If you are missing even one of them, you'll be impaired. All the parts are necessary.

If the whole body is the living roster of God's kingdom, then the parts are the individual members exercising their unique role in the kingdom. The Bible teaches that each of us is uniquely equipped by God to participate in the kingdom. This unique equipping is called a spiritual gift. A spiritual gift is a God-given enabling that lets each member contribute to building the kingdom. It is not to be confused with natural abilities, temperament, or learned skills. It is also different from a passion or interest. It is an enabling that is given and powered by God.

During one potluck night when nearly everyone seemed to bring a side dish, one of the members of the group said, "This would probably work out a lot better if you told us all what to bring." This is where the metaphor breaks down. There is a lot of luck in potluck, but there is none in the body of Christ. In the body we do have a leader who not only tells us what we are to bring to the table, but actually gives it to us. Spiritual gifts are not abilities that we choose ourselves and work hard to bring up to standard. They are given by God for specific purposes. Paul says that spiritual gifts are "manifestation of the Spirit" that are "given for the common good" (1 Cor. 12:7). These empowerments of God are vital to the Christian community. They allow us to serve in the specific ways that God intended.

When we enter into discipling or other intentional relationships with GenXers, we should always have the goal of helping them understand and use their giftedness. Disciple making does not involve shaping people into our image, with our gifts and passions. Rather, it is helping an individual see God's unique craftsmanship in his life. God's handiwork is evident in the heart of every believer. That is why understanding spiritual gifts is an essential part of the discipling process.

Why Spiritual Gifts Are Important

They Show Us That God Loves Order

From the beginning God showed how much he loves order. He created something out of nothing and it was good. It had order and purpose. It was beautiful and it made sense. When man's rebellion entered the scene, the created order began to break apart. Order began to give way to chaos and disorder.

GenXers have inherited a world that is disordered. It seems almost random. But if God is summing up all things in Christ, he is also restoring order. An attribute of God is that he likes to put things in order.

One of the ways he does this is by putting order in the church, not just in his desire to have orderly worship and orderly interactions, but by actually putting the members of his church body into a cohesive arrangement. With spiritual gifts, the whole body is organized the way he wants it. Christ is the head of the body and we are the parts, all arranged into a meaningful order.

When all of the parts are functioning in the body of Christ, it works beautifully. Before our eyes, we see it

71

coming together. We experience the community of believers in motion—caring for each other, challenging each other, serving each other. When it works well, it is an amazing thing to witness and experience.

For GenXers raised in a disordered world, this experience is meaningful and powerfully real. We become living examples of how God is taking a fragmented world and knitting it back together. God takes disordered people and relationships and brings us into order as we live together in a purposeful community. God loves order and he demonstrates it by the way he puts our community together.

They Show How Every Individual Is Important

One of the astounding things about spiritual gifts is that they *all* are important. There is not one part of the body that we can do without. Paul writes, "Those parts of the body that seem to be weaker are indispensable, and the parts we think are less honorable we treat with special honor" (1 Cor. 12:22–23). We may have a body with gorgeous eyes, functional ears, and stinky feet, but every part has an important and unique role in the body. Even the parts that annoy us or pain us are crucial. The parts that are frequently overlooked or underappreciated also help us work well together as a body.

For GenXers who have never felt significant, this is a powerful doctrine. No one is disregarded. No one is unimportant. One GenXer said, "I think I have the gift of mercy. That's such a wimpy gift." Sorry, wrong answer! Mercy is a vitally important gift. If those with gifts of mercy did not step up to bat, our communities would be inadequate and important needs might go unmet.

Every gift is important. Every part is significant in completing the body. There are no wimpy gifts.

For other GenXers who are prone to apathy and underinvolvement, this teaching also becomes a powerful exhortation. One young man said, "I really like my church but I just don't think I can get involved." When asked why, he said that he didn't have time. GenXers are objectively busier than any previous generation but we all have some time for the things that are important to us. For a Christian, there should be nothing more important than building the kingdom. No Christian is given the option of sitting on the sidelines indefinitely. We are all called to exercise our gifts. When we are discipling GenXers, we should exhort them to become involved in some way that uses their gifts.

They Help Us Set Priorities

Jordan was in college when he realized that he probably had the spiritual gift of evangelism. He had an intense desire to share his faith with others and see his friends come into the kingdom. For him, talking about Jesus was easy and natural. He got plenty of confirmation that he was gifted in this area. During his freshman year, two guys in his dorm hall became believers with his help. He led an investigative Bible study his junior year that saw three people become believers. This pattern continued throughout his college years.

Knowing this, Jordan was able to set his spiritual priorities. He soaked up books and sermons on relational evangelism. He went to conferences like Urbana and attended other retreats where he could be taught and challenged. He focused his personal Bible study on understanding the gospel fully and examining how members of the early church shared their faith. Once out of college, he began volunteering with Young Life, a ministry that emphasizes building relationships with high school students who are not yet believers. He is a few years out of college and he still continues to shine.

Understanding your giftedness allows you to focus your efforts in your personal study, as well as in the direction of your spiritual growth and in the emphasis of your ministry. This helps set personal priorities and avoid distractions that might derail you. This kind of focus does not make you more narrow. It just makes you sharper. Like Jordan, knowing your giftedness can give you a sense of direction in your personal study and growth, as well as in your ministry.

They Help Us Receive Ministry from Others

Kurt has a gut-wrenching decision to make concerning a career move. He loves where he lives. He has a great church and an active ministry. But his job is going nowhere. Last week he got a call from an old college friend offering him a seemingly fantastic job in a city one thousand miles away where he doesn't know a single person. He called his former spiritual mentor, Richard, for advice. Kurt explained his dilemma well on the phone, but finally Richard said, "This is a huge decision. Can you drive down here this weekend so we can talk it over?" Kurt agreed and prepared himself for the short road trip.

Before he left, Kurt told a friend, "I know I need to do this, but to be honest, it scares me to death to go down there to see him."

His friend looked puzzled. "I thought you had a good relationship with him," he said.

"I do," said Kurt. "It's just that Richard can see right through me. All he has to do is take one look at me and he'll probably know my motives and everything else. He's amazing that way."

"Really?" asked his friend.

"Oh yeah. He does it all the time. He can walk into a room and meet someone and almost immediately know what their struggles are. It's sort of weird. With me, he hits the nail on the head every time. I'm kind of nervous about what I'll hear when I talk with him."

Whether or not Kurt could articulate that Richard possessed "discernment," he certainly had a keen awareness of the other man's giftedness. And because he knew this, he opened himself up to receiving ministry from him. The idea of talking with him about his future was a little unsettling—none of us like to have our motives fully exposed—but Kurt knew that this conversation would be an important part of his decision-making process. He knew God had equipped Richard for just such a task.

When we understand our own giftedness, we also begin to understand where we are deficient and how we can receive ministry from others. We begin to become aware of the value of other gifts. We let the prophets confront us and the teachers teach us and the exhorters challenge us. We let the discerners expose us when we are proud; we let the merciful soothe us when we are hurting.

Understanding our own giftedness allows us to understand how others may be gifted as well. We begin to see the big picture and how we all play a part in it. Then we can allow ourselves to receive the gift ministries of others. We let our spiritual brothers and sisters do what God has uniquely equipped them to do.

They Help Build the Kingdom

We are living a Story about a King who uses workers, each with unique gifts and skills, to construct his kingdom. When we use our gifts, we participate in building the kingdom. It is vitally important for each believer to understand how he or she has been equipped by God to join in this process. We are part of something bigger than ourselves. We are literally constructing the kingdom of God in the hearts of men and women.

When we teach, exhort, serve, discern, show mercy, or do anything else to honor God with our gifts, we are furthering his kingdom. We become vital and active in his story. Narrative discipling involves helping the younger believer see the Story, then become part of the Story. We cannot fully participate in the Story without knowing the role that God has given us to play. This is why understanding and using our spiritual gifts is so important. In doing so, we play our part in the Story. We help build the kingdom of God.

Discovering Gifts

Over the years there has been a lot of discussion about how to discover your spiritual gifts. Books and seminars give us great systems and strategies. But to be honest, uncovering spiritual gifts is not like an Easter egg hunt where you have to look under the cushions or behind all the furniture. The goodies are not hidden from us. Instead, the candy is usually in plain sight. For most believers, a spiritual gift is the most obvious possibility. The discipler's job is to see the potential giftedness of the disciple and nurture it.

Watch for hints of giftedness. Examine your conversations and observations for the signs. Does she have uncanny insight into people? Is she drawn to the left-out members of the group? Can he present truths clearly and compellingly? Does he always set up the chairs for a meeting without having to be asked? In time you will see patterns emerge and then you can share your insights and speculations with your disciple. Giftedness may be revealed in the passions expressed by the individual. Passions are not the same as gifts but they often give you clues as to how the giftedness might manifest itself. One GenXer had a passion for prison ministry at a women's penitentiary. When her motives were explored, it became evident that her desire was for these women to know Jesus. In two months, three of these women had come to know Christ in response to her ministry. Her passion was prison ministry, but her gift was evangelism. The prison ministry was the vehicle for exercising her gift.

Gifts are also revealed by confirming ministry experiences. If the person is clearly affirmed in a ministry, then consider the possibility that he is exercising his gifts. Remember Jordan? He understood his giftedness by his passion for sharing his faith, as well as in the confirmation he got when he did it.

We can also use tools to assist us in identifying spiritual gifts. One commonly used tool is a spiritual gifts questionnaire. Kenneth Cain Kinghorn and others have developed these instruments that have proven to be helpful guides for many people.[1] We have included one of our own in the Discipler's Tool Kit at the end of the book. Feel free to copy it and use it as a resource in your discipling. However, when you use it, be discerning. Having a high score on one scale does not necessarily signify the presence of a spiritual gift, nor does a low score indicate the absence of a gift. Spiritual gift questionnaires are merely guides to direct and focus your thinking. They are not authoritative by themselves.

As a discipler, there are times when a person's giftedness is not clear to you, even after several conversations and the use of spiritual gift questionnaires and other methods. When this happens, make sure that you first examine yourself. Ask yourself these questions: Where is my own relationship with God? Am I close enough to him to hear from him? Have I been faithful in prayer? Is there any area of habitual sin that may be causing me to be blinded to spiritual realities? Am I trying to mold this person into my own image? Do I know this person well enough to make a good judgment?

On the other hand, there may be some hindrances in the individual's own life that inhibit the exercise of his or her gift. The hindrances may be obvious, like sexual immorality, hostility, or prejudice. They may be more subtle, though. They may be a comfortable lifestyle or a busy schedule. Whatever the hindrance, it must be cleared away if it keeps the individual from using her gifts to honor God. As a discipler, we probe these hindrances and exhort the younger believer toward change.

Finally, don't get hung up on determining the exact name for the gift. Sometimes people debate whether or not the gifts are exhaustively mentioned in Scripture. That is to say, are *all* of the gifts mentioned by name in the Bible? The debate essentially boils down to semantics. Whether someone has the gift of counseling or insists on calling it exhortation is not the point. It is what it is. The gift is however God chooses to equip the individual believer. The label scarcely matters. If it looks like a duck, and quacks like a duck, and smells like a duck, then it must be a duck. If you want to call it a water fowl instead, then go right ahead. Just don't hold it down when it wants to take off. It does not matter what you call the gift, as long as you know what it looks like when it's in use.

What Are Gift Mixes?

A few Christian thinkers have come up with the interesting notion of a "gift mix" or a "giftedness set."

These usually involve an understanding of how natural abilities, learned abilities, and spiritual gifts all combine to form a cohesive mix. For example, Sharon has an innate tendency to be creative; she also has acquired skills in art and a spiritual gift of service. We find her painting murals in the children's Sunday school classrooms and helping the church create beautiful banners for its foyer.

Mike was born with a natural athleticism. He has learned how to play soccer well and he has the spiritual gift of mercy. We find him volunteering to coach soccer camps for inner-city kids.

These are just two examples of how natural abilities, learned abilities, and spiritual gifts all converge. The possible combinations of these mixes are nearly endless. In some models of gift mixes, the concept of dominant and supportive spiritual gifts is also proposed. A dominant gift is the lead gift. The supportive gifts strengthen the lead gift. For example, a person may have the dominant gift of exhortation with teaching and discernment as supportive gifts. The individual's ultimate goal is to exhort, to motivate. His ability to present truth clearly and to understand the hearts of his listeners strengthens his ability to exhort well.

Another person may have the dominant gift of administration. Her supportive gift of faith strengthens her ability to organize efforts that may seem hopeless or a waste of time. Her faith allows her to have a quiet assurance that God has a purpose in what he is leading her to organize.

Whether or not you endorse the concepts of gift mixes or dominant and supportive gifts, it should be abundantly clear that the expression of spiritual gifts is varied and complex. Two people may have the same spiritual gift but it may look quite different. Anyone who has been to a Billy Graham crusade has seen the gift of evangelism at work, but there are many with the same gift who will never lead people to the Lord in droves. Instead, their gift takes the form of building individual relationships and personally sharing their faith.

As you disciple an individual, it is probably less important that you map out his exact gift mix or identify his dominant and supportive gifts than it is to understand that the expression of gifts takes many forms. Spiritual gifts are not two-dimensional constructs. They are vibrant manifestations of God's Spirit lived out in three-dimensional reality.

Gifts and Universal Responsibilities

A college group was planning a short-term evangelism project to the beach during spring break. One member of the group said he was not going because he didn't have the gift of evangelism. This raises an interesting point. If God has gifted some people for some specific purposes, such as teaching or evangelism, then should we all feel compelled to do these things?

Usually the answer to this is yes! While one person may be empowered by God to be an evangelist, we are all mandated by God to share our faith. Just because a person does not have the spiritual gift of mercy does not release him from the responsibility to act mercifully to those in need. A person without the spiritual gift of administration can still be organized. The lack of a spiritual gift of giving does not free you up from your tithe.

This is not contradictory to the notion that our gifts direct our ministry. However, all Christians are called to live out their faith completely. Spiritual gifts give us focus and direction, but we still have a responsibility to show complete obedience to God.

We are wise not to lose sight of the one obvious fact: These manifestations of the Spirit, these enablings of God, are gifts. They are another example of how the God of the universe chooses to show his love for us. He cares about us individually; he picks out just the right gift for each of us. Yet he cares about us corporately by arranging the gifts so that they all fit together. God is the giver of good gifts.

She's calling for help, for attention, so God and I give it to her. I just talk to her and she just listens. God makes sense. I just want her to give it one more try. So many people need God. He's the answer to all our problems yet so few are willing to take that step and jump into God's arms. I want to be used by God in whatever way possible. If he can use me now when I'm still so far from what I should be, who knows what he can do later on in my life.

PART 2

FAITH

An Awesome God

7

I've experienced God and his love in the hardest times of my life. He's walked with me when I was alone and confused, held on to me in my greatest anger, and waited patiently for me to come back when I shook my fist at him and the world.

Head versus Heart?

Danny was a new Christ-follower with enthusiasm to burn. His life before Christ had been full of substance abuse; shallow relationships; thoughtless, commitment-free sex; and lots of despair. His new life as a Christian seemed different in every way. He was involved in real community for the first time. His drug habit had lost nearly all of its allure. The Bible seemed to be a living thing, its words jumping off the page and into his heart. He prayed for long periods of time and couldn't seem to worship enough. He greeted each day with joy and a rising sense of hopefulness that God was up to something good and that it involved Danny's own life.

Tom was committed to discipling Danny and encouraging him in his new faith. Tom helped Danny learn the spiritual disciplines of prayer, fasting, Scripture reading, meditation, and service. He helped Danny see his old and new relationships in the light of God's Story and he watched as Danny made apologies and restitution, experienced reconciliation, and built deep friendships. At each turn, Danny responded to Tom's gentle leadership with eager openness and a humble, submissive spirit.

After some time Tom decided that it was important that Danny be grounded in the essential teachings of the Christian faith. He proposed that he and Danny devote a biweekly meeting to studying the basics of Christian doctrine, which Tom believed would give structure and context to Danny's voracious Bible reading. For the first time, Danny balked.

"I don't understand why I need to learn *theology,* of all things," Danny protested. "Theology is for professors and old people, for preachers and people with big-time control issues."

"Maybe that's true for some," replied Tom, "but we still need a way to think about God, some basic beliefs about who he is."

Danny shook his head in disagreement. "The best I can tell, theology tries to put God in a box, to limit his power by explaining him. And the problem with doctrine is that it sets up an us-versus-them situation. It makes people feel that those who disagree with them are wrong."

Tom paused to try to find common ground. After a moment he said, "It doesn't have to be that way, Danny. But it is important for us to have a disciplined way of thinking about God, to know and love him with our minds."

"What I need," replied Danny, "is to know Jesus in my heart, to have a relationship with him that isn't limited by a bunch of doctrines and beliefs. I know I have to know some theology but I want to know the bare minimum—who Jesus is and why it matters. Tom, I'd rather spend my time hanging out with others in the community, praying and worshiping with them and serving the poor than studying theology. Thanks, but no thanks."

In his preference for relationship over doctrine, for practical service rather than theological precision, Danny is not an unusual Xer. Perhaps no other generation has been so disinterested in a systematic exploration of the Christian faith. The tendency to see theological reflection and practical devotion as incompatible partners is not new with our generation, however. Builders and Silents (the generation between the Builders and Boomers) were interested in the nuts and bolts of theology, packing churches for expositional preaching, prophecy conferences, and week-long Bible-teaching marathons. Boomers en masse rejected such emphasis, preferring preaching that addressed felt needs and emotional struggles. In the space of a generation, we witnessed a change in taste that could be symbolized by these sermon titles: "The Second Coming According to Daniel and Revelation" and "How to Have a Fulfilling Marriage."

Older generations wanted content and Bible knowledge, preferring to be left to themselves to apply the teachings of the Bible to their lives: *Is it true?* Boomers demanded practical application: *Does it work for me?* Generation Xers are asking a fundamentally different question: *Does it matter?*

Our generation demands that teaching be relevant to the real-life struggles inherent in surviving in a dangerous world where nobody may know your name. We are not interested in knowledge for the sake of knowledge.

We disdain the therapeutic culture that demands that preaching meet each individual's emotional needs. We see a world that needs fixing and lives that are torn and we want a faith that matters, that addresses in plain language our struggles, heartaches, and dreams. We want to know Jesus with our hearts, and it is not so important, we think, that we understand him with our minds. No, we are not much interested in theology.

Head and Heart

At first glance our preference for heart over head, for relationship over practical knowledge, seems admirable. But it is tough to love without thinking about the one you love. When we fall in love or choose to love a friend, we do so because we are drawn to something in that person and, inevitably, we can articulate why this is so. "I love her because of her joyful spirit and sensitivity to those who are hurting." "I love him because he is powerful and gentle at the same time." "I love my friend because she is loyal and encouraging but is not afraid to confront me when I need it."

At some level every relationship outside of cheap romance novels involves thought and reflection if it is to last and to grow. As couples who have been married for many years attest, we can never fathom a person to his or her depths. There is always more to learn, much more to discover. The conflict between head and heart in love is needless. This is all the more the case with our relationship with God.

If we are to have a growing relationship with God, we have to think and learn about him. We have to come to grips with his character and values. We need to know how he interacts with others and what he tells us about himself. This, by definition, is theology.

88

Many have made the following observation, which is no less true because of its simplicity: We all have a theology whether we admit it or not; the only question is whether or not our theology is good or bad, true or false.

Each Xer we disciple has a theology, whether or not he knows it. Given the postmodern climate and the impact of media on our generation, the chances are good that this theology is disjointed, internally inconsistent, and even contradictory. We can be almost sure that an Xer's theology is not as neat and systematic as his grandfather's may have been. And we can also assume that an Xer will see this cognitive messiness as a virtue.

Sloppy theology makes for a bad narrative, however. Unless we can help Xers link their lives with the Story that is ordered and coherent, their own lives will be disjointed and inconsistent. Our theology provides the narrative structure for the story of our lives.

The Story

Sources of the Story

The first question faced by theologians is: What are our sources? Which body or bodies of truth and wisdom will we draw on?

For Christ-followers there is one supreme source—the Bible, the covenant document in which God tells the Story of his love relationship with his people and his consummate quest to create a new community of people for himself prior to his creation of a new heaven and new earth. The Bible understood as the only wholly reliable source of God's heart, character, and actions is our primary source. But it will not be the only one.

Protestant Christians have long been critical of Roman Catholics for their placing church tradition and history on a par with the Bible. This critique is well-founded when tradition supersedes or contradicts the teaching of Scripture. But it is possible to overreact by writing off entirely the use of tradition. While tradition and history are not wholly reliable sources of God's character, they are confirmatory evidence of the teaching of Scripture. Furthermore, if God is Lord over history in general and the history of his new community in particular, we can expect that tradition and history will reveal something of God's heart to us.

The spirituality of the new community is a particularly helpful source for its theology. "The integration of theology and spirituality," writes Stanley Grenz, ". . . means that theology must arise out of the life of the believing community. That is, theology must flow from discipleship. Theology is not merely the intellectual findings of professional thinkers, but requisite knowledge for doers-disciples of the Lord who need to know whom they are following and why they are following him."[1]

It is important for us to draw on these rich sources of knowledge about God's Story. The Story of God's new community, which is our Story, will contain much of relevance for our own lives, and we will speak more of this later.

Structure of the Story

Christian theology is both static and dynamic. It is static because it contains a fixed body of unchangeable truth, affirmations that are true for all times, all places, and all cultures. In general, Christians have agreed that, while there are many nonessential components of the community's faith, there is also a core of essential doctrines that must never be compromised. These are the affirmations that form and sustain the community and provide its reason for being and its mission.

On the other hand, most Christians have realized that the ways in which we understand and communicate this core of truth can and must change depending on the time and culture. Certain cultures, certain stretches of time, and even certain historical events demand varying presentations of the gospel. ~~Each generation of Christ-followers is charged with reinterpreting the gospel anew for its own generation.~~

We must do this for the Xers we are discipling. To do so we have to understand four things: the core of truth we want to communicate, the history of the community that has been faithful to this truth, the times in which we live, and the particular ways in which the gospel becomes good news for the individual we are discipling. Frankly this is not an easy task. ~~It demands that we be not only students of theology, but also students of culture and the human heart, even a certain individual human heart.~~ Given that, we must learn to think and communicate theological truth using themes that resonate in our heart and the hearts of those we are discipling.

The theological themes of community, reconciliation, and hope can form the structure for a theological vision that will capture the hearts and minds of Generation X Christ-followers. Under the rubric of these three themes, we can express the essential components of the core body of theological truth. The theme of community speaks to the character of the triune God, who exists in perfect community, as well as to his creative activity. The theme of reconciliation captures the drama of the fall of man as well as God's stunning redemption of men and women through the life, death, and resurrection of Christ; reconciliation also speaks to the ways in which we live out practically the implications of Christ's life, death, and resurrection. And the theme of hope, which we will develop fully in part 3, provides an eschatological vision of what it means to live with integrity and purpose in this particular moment of history.

God in Three Persons

Theology that is faithful to the Bible and to the story of the church begins with God himself, who is the source of life and the creator of all that exists. The character and nature of God is an astounding mystery, a thing full of wonder. Somehow most systematic theology textbooks manage to kill the lion, if not from irrelevance, then from boredom. A typical way to approach the character of God is by listing his attributes—love, holiness, omniscience, and so on. These are important themes, to be sure, but they are usually presented with all the interest and drama of the mutual-fund listings in the newspaper.

The character of each Person of the Trinity speaks to Xers profoundly. The all-powerful and wise Father contrasts with the failings of the human fathers of the most-aborted generation in history, many of whom probably grew up in a broken home. The Person of the Son—Jesus Christ—is a deeply attractive figure to Xers. He spoke plainly, lived authentically, placed himself with the marginalized and disenfranchised, challenged the system, and cared for the poor. He is the most compelling figure in history for all generations.

The Person of the Holy Spirit can be extraordinarily meaningful to our generation. In between his historical evangelical status as the "forgotten member of the Trinity" and the fringe charismatic emphasis on the gifts of the Spirit to the exclusion of the Father and the Son lies the importance of the Holy Spirit as "the experienced, empowering return of God's own personal presence in and among us," in Gordon Fee's helpful phrase.[2]

In a culture that often provokes feelings of alienation and to members of a generation often forced to raise itself, the image and truth of a God who is radically and faithfully present with his people are deeply resonant. This is a God who is not silent and does not leave us as orphans.

Perhaps the fundamental truth to understand about the person of God is that he exists in relationship. This is about all we can know with certainty about the doctrine of the Trinity—that God is one in essence and three in person. This triune God exists in perfect community, which means that relationships are more important than anything else and that we have a model for what relationships can look like.

There is a deep hunger in our generation for meaningful relationships, for community. Accompanying this hunger is a corresponding inability to develop and deepen real relationships. Careful disciplers of Xers will not miss the opportunity to explore the very nature of God himself as a model for community.

Xers tend to be deeply curious about God. This is in contrast to Boomers, who tend to be deeply concerned with what God can do for them. God is not a boring subject for our generation, but traditional discussions about God's attributes or endless speculations about his nature are tedious for a generation used to sound bites. It's not that we don't want to think—the critiques of too many evangelical Boomer authors to the contrary—it's that we want to think about things that matter, things that speak to life as we know it. One such thing that matters is the doctrine of creation.

The fact that God created the world has implications for all of life. God, who creates, exists in community, and creativity flows out of relationship, the rich, dynamic interplay of Father, Son, and Holy Spirit. The Father creates all things for the Son, and the Spirit animates all of creation. All of the created order belongs to this God-in-community.

Crowning creation was man and woman, made in the image of God, carrying something of his personality. They were assigned a prominent place in creation, responsible as stewards for the maintenance and care of all God had made. Very soon after the creation of the man, God made the woman as his partner, his soul—and body—mate. God not only exists in community but builds community and relationship into the very fabric of creation.

The doctrine of creation teaches us about God's sovereignty and creativity. All things owe their existence to and are dependent on God. He is the only self-sufficient being in all of creation. He does not owe his existence to any other factor. This all-powerful God is in control. As he reveals in the rest of the Story, he can be trusted. Life is not randomness but is patterned and given texture by a good Creator.

The doctrine of creation teaches us about the significance of men and women. We were made by God, in his image, to be his stewards and representatives. We are highly dignified, significant in God's plan, and beautiful. Our proper relation to God is as his friends, servants, and agents. We carry the weight and privilege of carrying out his will on earth. In a culture in which infanticide and euthanasia are spoken of as viable alternatives to living with illness or deformity, we can speak of the dignity of all men and women. To a generation sometimes convinced of the randomness and meaninglessness of life, we can speak of our high place and destiny in God's creation.

And the doctrine of creation speaks to the importance of the creation itself. The doctrine gives environmentalism—such a critical issue for many Xers—its reason for being. While the Bible clearly separates the creation from the Creator, it also clearly pronounces creation good and communicates the gravity of men and women's responsibility to be caretakers and stewards of all that God has made.

Fixing Broken Things

As the Story progressed, the plot darkened. Men and women chose to worship the idol of self-sufficiency and power rather than the true God—they fell from their perfect state of community with the Creator and became instruments of destruction to themselves, each other, and the creation.

The bottom line is that the community has become fractured. Our relationship with God is broken, as are our relationships with others and with the created order. We don't have to work too hard to convince Xers of the reality of sin; they are not given to utopian dreams of the perfectibility of man, in spite of the relentless self-esteem drills they were forced to endure in grade school. Xers do not theorize about relational brokenness; they live in it day after day. Xer literature and music describe the feelings of being a stranger in a strange land, of being homesick for a home we never had, and of despairing of finding real relationships. We cap this with a cynical spin ("It's the end of the world as we know it, and I feel fine," sang REM's Michael Stipe in a generational anthem) but beneath the irony and denial our loneliness and alienation hurt us deeply.

The theme of reconciliation permeates both Old and New Testaments. The covenant God of the Old Testament pursues his people with white-hot intensity, remaining faithful in the face of their faithlessness, and offering chance after chance for restored relationship. Read in context, many of the most furious prophetic denunciations of Israel's apostasy sound not so much like angry tyranny as they do the grievings of a rejected Lover. We are told that God's character is that of one who "tries to bring us back when we have been separated from him" (2 Sam. 14:14 NLT).

In the New Testament we see Jesus weeping over the city he loves and longs to see return to him. We see his life, in which he modeled and taught reconciliation; his death, in which he paid for reconciliation; and his resurrection, in which he sealed and made available the reconciliation of men and women to God. The role of followers of Christ, particularly leaders, is to be agents of reconciliation, "as though God were making his appeal through us. . . . Be reconciled to God" (2 Cor. 5:20). And the closing book of the Bible, the Revelation, speaks again and again of a new reconciled community where divisions and warfare are past and people of every people group, culture, and language are united in eternal praise to God. Reconciliation of God to man, man to man, and man to created order is clearly the goal for which God is summing up all things in Christ, bringing all things together under his lordship.

The doctrine of reconciliation has considerable practical and ethical consequences. If the intent of God's plan is to reconcile all things to Christ and if our task is to imitate God by being agents of reconciliation, then our communities will be places where reconciliation is expected and modeled. This will include reconciliation between ethnic and racial groups, as well as interpersonal and familial reconciliation. Most important for a discipler of Xers, the doctrine of reconciliation provides a place within the Story for members of our generation to locate themselves. We know intuitively that we need to be reconciled to God and to others. The Story explains how we came to be alienated, provides a hero who made reconciliation possible, and offers a vision for hope and healing in shattered relationships.

Trusting in the Future

According to Paul and the other New Testament writers, the cardinal Christian virtues, like God himself, exist in a trinity: faith, hope, and love. As Paul in particular develops his theology of these virtues, it becomes clear that hope is the foundation and root of all of Christian practice, the deep wellspring from which faith and love flow. This is so because Christian hope springs from a profoundly eschatological vision of creation, a comprehensive picture of what God has done, is doing, and will do in history. In part 3, we will develop these theological implications at greater length.

We all have a theology whether or not we know we do; the only question concerns whether or not our theology is a true one. Thinking about God is unavoidable, and to avoid doing so is undesirable. Effective disciplers of Xers will themselves possess a theological vision and be able to articulate to those whom they disciple the wisdom and practical benefit of thinking theologically. A vision of God rooted in community, reconciliation, and hope provides order in a dislocated world and a sense of home for a homeless generation.

The Spiritual Disciplines for a New Generation

I really need to get away from all the confusion. It controls me. It eats at me. It fills my mind. I need quiet.

A Lack of Discipline

"No matter what I try," said Heather, "I just can't seem to concentrate on praying and reading the Bible. I try to go back to all the methods I was taught in Sunday school, but they just don't seem to work for me anymore. I know that my relationship with Jesus is supposed to be real and alive—it's a *relationship* after all—but I just can't seem to connect."

Bill's experience is similar to Heather's, though his background is different. "When I was growing up, my parents talked about spirituality a lot. They had both been into the '60s scene, with all of the gurus and the Eastern philosophy, so they were real open to stuff. They talked about life forces and tapping into positive energy and finding your own spiritual path. It sounded great but it was always so abstract, so subjective, that I could never seem to dial into their experiences for myself. Then I became a Christian and I thought that I would really understand what it meant to be spiritual. The problem is, all of the teaching I get emphasizes either following formulas or feeling feelings. I find it hard to pray like someone else says I should and I want to know what the Bible says about God and life, not spend a lot of time asking 'what does this mean to you?'"

Heather and Bill share a condition with countless other young adult Christians—a lack of connection with God, at least in their daily life. On the one hand, they are faced with the traditional church, which has emphasized rote methods of Bible reading and memorization, prayer, and meditation. On the other hand, they live in the midst of an experience-based culture, which encourages them to explore their own feelings in exhaustive detail and to pursue a vaguely defined personal spirituality. Young adults are able to talk the language of spiritual experience, but these experiences, which are largely devoid of spiritual content, leave them unfulfilled and hungry for a depth of relationship and intimacy with God.

Theologian Alister McGrath has observed that the lack of a compelling vision of Christian spirituality is one of the weaknesses of evangelical Protestantism. In fact, "if there is any long-term threat to the future of evangelicalism, it may well be its lack of attention to spirituality."[1] In response, there is a growing trend away from traditional expressions of faith and toward faith communities that are more image- and experience-based. Some Christians are moving from evangelicalism toward Anglicanism, Roman Catholicism, and even Eastern Orthodoxy, traditions characterized by a rich appreciation for image and a strong tradition of mystical experience.

Other evangelicals, committed to their theological distinctives, are looking to capture deeper spiritual experience as well. Much attention has centered on the classical spiritual disciplines of prayer, solitude, Bible reading, meditation, and fasting as means to achieving greater intimacy with God. The popularity of recent discussions of the spiritual disciplines, such as those of Richard Foster, indicate that there is a growing hunger among evangelicals to experience more of the presence and power of God.[2]

As we have said, many Xers want to experience God directly, free of doctrine and psychology. While it is impossible to separate our knowledge of God or self from our experience of God, it is important that we honor the hunger of many in our generation to enter deeply into relationship with God.

The classical spiritual disciplines offer this sort of experience-oriented life of faith, while they gently and almost imperceptibly nudge those who practice them toward understanding God and self. They are an effective starting point for pursuing a life of faith, accessible to all who will rely on God's grace to bring discipline to the pursuit of relationship with him. Some of the classical disciplines are of particular relevance to our generation, and we will explore these. This chapter will focus on practical application of the spiritual disciplines. Before we can lead others into the disciplines, we must first experience them ourselves.

Solitude and Quiet

The movie *Jerry Maguire* featured actor Tom Cruise as a twentysomething sports agent moving through a frantic life of deal making and breaking. At his bachelor party shortly before his wedding, Jerry's friends showed a video they had produced featuring brief interviews with the groom-to-be's former girlfriends. Each woman agreed that one of Jerry's chief characteristics was that "He can't stand to be alone." When he was forced to be by himself, Jerry was less than himself. In truth, he had no self that was separate from his relationships.

The fictional Jerry Maguire's story is similar to the stories of many other Xers. Stimulated by television and music, raised on video games at the mall, left to run in packs of latchkey kids, we have seldom been alone. Xers tend to define themselves as part of a group. More than one observer has noted that Xers formulate morality in the context of a group; while Builders would stand on the moral principles of their forebears and Boomers would follow the dictates of their private conscience, Xers tend to arrive at moral consensus in the company of friends.

We live in a noisy culture that grows louder all of the time. We don't know what it means to be quiet or even to be in a quiet place, and when we do happen along silence and solitude, we are not sure that we like it.

But Christians have always experienced God in silence and solitude. From the biblical writers to the desert fathers to medieval monastic communities to contemporary mystics, the Christian witness is that God often reveals himself in the lonely places, when we can quiet our hearts enough to hear him.

Henri Nouwen made the helpful distinction between loneliness and solitude.[3] Loneliness is the consequence of being alone in the company of others, of living life surrounded by people but apart from community, of failing to listen to our heart longings and disappointments. Solitude is being content to be alone because we know

102

that we are not really alone. Solitude has very little to do with whether or not we are in the presence of others, but everything to do with our being centered and whole whether alone or surrounded by other people. "Loneliness," writes Richard Foster, "is inner emptiness. Solitude is inner fulfillment."[4]

Our generation knows much of loneliness and very little of solitude. In fact we tend to see solitude, or at least the experience of being alone, as the cause of loneliness. Like Jerry Maguire, we do everything possible to avoid being alone. Yet growth begins in solitude, in the lonely places where God can be heard over the incessant chatter of media and the intrusive noise of crowds and the confused protests of our own hearts.

How do we find solitude while living in a crowded, high-volume culture? How do we find solitude when our generation has been raised to believe that aloneness is the enemy? We find it by the stark, simple act of creating space for quiet and for God and daring to listen to his voice.

A first attempt at solitude for Xers had best be a drastic one. If you can, get away for an hour with nothing but a Bible and a notebook, read a bit, write and reflect a bit, and then listen. Then write what you hear. Don't try to tell God too much. Concentrate on what he may have to say to you. This will be hard at first. It is not easy to quiet the inner voices that will clamor for attention. Do your best to ignore them.

Next, try to find moments of solitude in the middle of a life surrounded by people. Perhaps you will find this in your car, or late at night, or very early in the morning. Try to create some little space in every day simply to be quiet and still and alone. One friend of ours goes to a busy McDonald's and sits for hours with an open Bible (guaranteeing that no one will approach him!) and a large Coke. He is in the middle of a crowd, but alone with God and his own heart.

The discipline of solitude will grow on you, and eventually you will jealously guard your solitary time. You will find that you are more composed and relaxed and centered. You will find that you can listen better to others. You will hear God more clearly. You will be ready to grow in some of the other disciplines.

Scripture

A devotion to the Bible is one of the defining characteristics of the Christian evangelical movement. It is also one of the most abused. Left to our own devices, we are apt to turn the Bible into an "owner's manual for life," as if God were concerned primarily with helping us navigate the rough waters of life with minimal discomfort. Worse, the Bible can be used to erect walls between us and others who don't share our view of its contents.

The Bible tells us that it is primarily a Story about God and the new community he is creating and about what he is doing in history. The Bible is about God, not us.

It is important that we receive the Bible as a Story and that we let its story become ours. This is not accomplished primarily by memorizing bits and pieces of the words of Scripture or becoming adept at pointing out proof texts that reinforce favored doctrines. The Story of the Bible becomes our story when we enter deeply into its stream, submit ourselves to all of its twists and turns and surprises, and long to see the passions and values of the Storyteller become our own. The Bible's Story becomes our own when we spend long, thoughtful hours in its company.

The ancient practice of *lectio divina* has proven to be helpful for many Xers in coming to experience the

Bible's Story. *Lectio divina* is simply a way of slowly reading, internalizing, and praying the Scriptures. There are four progressions in practicing *lectio divina*. First is the act of reading. This is not speed-reading or skimming, but rather a slow, repetitive savoring of the text. As you read, allow yourself to pause at words and phrases that strike you as significant. Second is the act of meditation, slowly repeating the text that you have just internalized by slow reading. "Chew" on the text as you repeat it, allowing its words to interact with your heart's dreams, fears, and hopes. Allow the words of the text to gently imprint themselves into your heart. Third, allow the read and meditated text to become prayer. Pray the very words of Scripture back to God, allowing them to become your words. You will find that your entire prayer life will be changed by this practice; it will become much richer and God—rather than self—focused. Fourth, spend time contemplating the text you have read, meditated on, and prayed. Be quiet and listen to what God is saying to your heart in light of the text.

Lectio divina is not easy at first. Like the discipline of solitude, it takes some getting used to for those who are comfortable with noise and for those who have previously regarded the Bible as something simply to be studied and memorized—*used*. But practiced well, *lectio divina* can become a taste of what God intends our lives to be like: a reflective experiencing of the presence of God.

It is important to note that *lectio divina* by itself does not meet all of our needs in terms of Scripture. Our culture tends to make even our Bible reading a subjective experience, primarily concerned with me—What does this mean to me? What is God telling me? It is important to study the Bible, to understand its original context and meaning, to allow it to shape our theological convictions and hence our lives. *Lectio divina* does not do away with the need for these important activities but

105

it does add an experiential dimension to our reading and praying of the Scriptures, which resonates in the hearts of many Xers.

Prayer

"We today yearn for prayer and hide from prayer," writes Richard Foster. "We believe prayer is something we should do, even something we want to do, but it seems like a chasm stands between us and actually praying. We experience the agony of prayerlessness."[5]

We doubt that anyone reading these words has failed to experience the agony of prayerlessness. Those raised in the evangelical tradition have had this agony heightened by the mythical dimension of prayer—the stories of great "prayer warriors"—and the legalistic dimension of prayer—the "quiet time."

Stories about great pray-ers such as E. M. Bounds, George Mueller, and Susannah Wesley may make great inspirational reading but they have plunged generations of young evangelicals into despair because their own lives do not match the lives of these especially called and gifted by God for prayer. And the great evangelical institution—the quiet time—has created similar discomfort and guilt for those who struggle to find daily time to pray.

When our lives are measured against unusually devout leaders and when spirituality is defined solely by one particular practice, we are tempted to flee to the hills, throw out a prayer or two when we can, and leave regular, intense, and meaningful communion with God to the spiritually elite. Xers in particular would rather flee than once again risk disappointment with themselves.

Providentially, the Bible's perspective on prayer creates freedom rather than guilt. Biblical prayer is vast in its variety. It is attuned to particular situations and always relationally based. It is God-centered in its motivation, form, and function. Most strikingly, prayer is our *response* to God rather than our desperate attempt to initiate a relationship with God, gaining his attention and earning his approval.

For thousands of years the foundational prayers for God's covenant people have been the Psalms. More than devotional reading designed to get us into a frame of mind and heart to pray, the Psalms themselves are the prayer book of the church, comprising the very words of our best prayers. Eugene Peterson is characteristically to the point: "If we wish to develop in the life of faith, to mature in our humanity, and to glorify God with our entire heart, mind, soul, and strength, the Psalms are necessary. We cannot bypass the Psalms."[6]

The Psalms range over the whole of the human experience, taking us from the heights of intoxication with God and his ways to the bitterest depths of loneliness, betrayal, and despair. The Psalms along with the prayer Jesus gave to his followers (Matt. 6:9–13) are the starting point for those who want to learn how to pray and for those who long to deepen their experience of prayer.

Perhaps the best pattern for psalm-praying is to pray consecutively through the Psalms, taking five a day. This will move one through the entire Psalter in one month. Many psalm-pray-ers find that dividing the five daily psalms into morning and evening prayer (like the Episcopal *Book of Common Prayer*) is helpful.

Like each of the disciplines we are considering, this may be a bit awkward at first. Our culture values self-expression above most anything else, and so the idea of praying another's words feels strange or perhaps even inauthentic. We will not have experienced the emotions conveyed in some of the words we will be praying.

But this is good for several reasons. It is good because these words are God's words and they indicate how he wants us to pray. And it is good because we are then able to pray in community with others, as the Lord brings to mind those whom we know in our own lives or those about whom we have heard or those in the persecuted church, who are experiencing today the emotions and struggles of the Psalm we are praying. This is good because it takes our focus off ourselves and puts it on God and others. We will find that the result of our psalm-praying will be that when we do pray using our own words, these words have a new depth and richness and broadness.

Praying the Psalms leads us into praying in community, which is another key way that prayer can become powerful for our generation. As we have said, the Bible talks very little about "me and Jesus." It talks a great deal about "us and Jesus." Jesus came to call us into a new and interdependent community, which strikes at the heart of our cultural individualism, not to mention our prayer life. Time alone with God is vitally important. But prayer in community, prayer with others, is equally important. In those times that the church has been most vital, its common life has been characterized by little cells of believers coming together to pour out their hearts to God in worship and praise and adoration, in anguish and hopelessness, in hope and anticipation, for and with each other.

In small groups centered around praise and intercessory prayer, many Xers begin to hope and to find healing and the strength to face life in a fractured world.

Fasting

At least on the face of it, fasting—the abstention from food for spiritual purposes—would seem to have little appeal to contemporary Americans, particularly Xers. We are the most affluent culture in history, and the value of instant gratification has deep roots in our collective heart. We are prone to believe that we ought to have, consume, and acquire more, not less. Our generation is characterized by its immediacy and impatience. A discipline such as fasting, which is at its core about self-denial and perseverance, would seem to have less than a fighting chance of gaining widespread acceptance.

Surprisingly there has been a resurgence of interest in the discipline of fasting in recent years, accompanied by a new interest in living a simple life. It appears that there is a considerable backlash against the American ethos of consumerism and a sense that the most real and lasting things may not be found by material gain and growth.

Jesus seemed to assume that his followers would fast (Matt. 6:16); his only concern was that they not publicly make a big deal of it. Spurred by this expectation of our Lord, we will want to fast. Our questions will be why? and how?

We should fast if for no other reason than Jesus said to do so. But there are many more reasons to practice this discipline. Fasting makes us aware that we are weak and dependent creatures. Fasting tends to sharpen our prayers and thoughts, giving them clarity and depth. It is both helpful and frightening that fasting tends to expose the prevalent sins in our heart. If we are prone to anger and impatience, fasting will bring these out. If we are given to lust, we may find our thoughts darker than usual. If we are given to envy, we will be jealous of those who are eating! If we are prideful, we will be quite impressed with ourselves for fasting and a bit contemptuous of those whose spiritual commitment comes just short of our own!

Fasting is a particularly relevant discipline for Xers for at least three reasons. First, it is a discipline that can be practiced in community. Churches, small groups, and groups of friends who fast together for spiritual growth, for help in making a difficult decision, or to seek God's direction find that their hearts are often knit more closely together. Second, fasting counters many of the cultural assumptions of our generation and so helps us to get to a more objective place where we can examine our heart and motivations with a ruthless eye. Third, the Bible ties the discipline of fasting with God's heart for justice and his concern for the oppressed and marginalized—aspects of his character that are meaningful to our generation.

> Is not this the kind of fasting I have chosen:
> to loosen the chains of injustice
>   and untie the cords of the yoke,
> to set the oppressed free
>   and break every yoke?
> Is it not to share your food with the hungry
>   and to provide the poor wanderer with shelter—
> when you see the naked, to clothe him,
> and not to turn away from your own flesh and blood?
>   Isaiah 58:6–7

In *Celebration of Discipline* Richard Foster has given excellent practical guidelines for fasting.[7] For our purposes it is enough to say that it is good to begin to practice the discipline a little at a time (perhaps a twenty-four-hour fast, followed by a thirty-six-hour fast, and then a longer one) and in community, if at all possible.

Worship

The end result of the disciplines, the goal of the Christian life, is that we worship God with more intensity, purity, and skill. Worship has both a private and public dimension, as illustrated by the Psalms.

The Psalms are intensely personal, springing from a meditative heart and based on real-life personal experiences. In the most inward Psalms, we are made to feel almost uncomfortable, as if we are intruding into private spaces of another's heart. But the Psalms were written for use in a corporate setting, for the very public worship of the covenant community! Worship is thus a profoundly private and a joyously public act.

Private worship comes when we come to grips with three things: the character and ways of God, our own heart's capacity to sin and turn from God, and God's grace in intersecting his Story with our story. Interior worship is focused on God. He is the point, not us. Our own lives are in view only inasmuch as they reveal the grace of God and as we acknowledge our dependence on him for all things.

Again the Psalms are the most helpful tools for cultivating private worship but they do not stand alone. The New Testament makes it clear that worship is an ethical activity. "I urge you . . . in view of God's mercy," wrote Paul, "to offer your bodies as living sacrifices, holy and pleasing to God—*this* is your spiritual act of worship" (Rom. 12:1, emphasis added). Worship is a way of life, not just a visible activity. We worship best when all of the details of our life are brought before Christ for evaluation, change, and recommitment. Worship is holistic, and those discipling Xers should have no problem communicating this integrated view of spirituality and life.

The public dimension of worship also resonates with Generation X. Worship always finds its most full expression in the context of community. The worshipers of the Old Testament praised God with joy and intensity. New Testament worshipers prayed, played, ate, and worshiped together. Throughout there is much emphasis on joy and loud music! Corporate worship is attractive to Xers, even worship that might feel a bit too expressive to older generations.

The distinction between "seeker services" and worship services is a helpful case in point. Following the lead of Willow Creek Community Church near Chicago, many churches concerned with reaching Baby Boomers fashioned public worship services that were targeted at non-Christians. Designed to remove all nonessential barriers to faith, the services are light on religious imagery, symbolism, jargon, and other traditional expressions of faith. For many Baby Boomers, seeker services were and are attractive, leading to a willingness to consider the claims of Christianity in a new way. Ideally, a seeker comes to faith through seeker services and then takes her place in the worshiping community.

It's a great strategy to reach a generation like the Boomers, who are apt to draw lines between public behavior and private faith. It is not at all a helpful strategy for Generation X. Our generation longs to experience God and is open to the transcendent. We're not afraid of the supernatural or the experiential. Authentic, vibrant, and even expressive worship that is not weird, forced, or alienating is a draw to Xers.

The key is worship that is hospitable and inviting, focused on God but warm to the outsider. Always the door must be kept open and the porch lights on. Xer worship that is attractive to non-Christians will be warm, joyful, interactive, full of music and a variety of forms of artistic expression, free of jargon or other "insider" behavior, and above all concerned with God and how he intersects with life. Worship is a vital part of the life of the new community and a prime way in which the community adds to itself.

The best worship is a personal interaction with the God who is telling the Story of the new community he is forming for himself. Like the Psalms, this worship will rehearse the story of the community in light of the Storyteller's faithful acts. And having rehearsed the story and worshiped the Storyteller together, the community moves out into the world determined to worship him with every part of its life.

God, this is the way I want to feel. I pray that I will keep my body and mind clean so that you can abide in a clean space in my heart. And thank you God for sticking with me even though I seem to justify so many wrong things in my life. Please keep pointing out these sins and help me clean them up.

PART 3

HOPE

9

A REASON FOR HOPE

We have lost a vision of God and his kingdom. This is my sorrow. This is my sadness. And this is my pain. But in the midst of this pain which these thoughts provoke, I find hope. My hope relies on a God who forgives me and still accepts me in the midst of my sin. Because of my relationship with him, I have been unconditionally forgiven and can spend eternity in his care. I want people to see this so bad. My hope is that not one person that I come in contact with will not experience at least a little piece of God. And not one person that I develop a meaningful relationship with will be able to walk away without a new curiosity or have their minds jarred. That is my hope.

Hope, Hopelessness, or Schizophrenia?

Try as she might, Julie couldn't figure Beth out. The two women had been meeting for several months now, after Beth asked Julie to help her grow in her faith and in her practice of the spiritual disciplines. Julie was fifteen years older than Beth but believed they would have much in common. Now she wasn't so sure.

Mostly Julie couldn't figure out if Beth was a hopeful person or a hopeless person. Julie had discipled many other women over the years. Usually she was able to identify whether or not another woman had hope in God's love and sovereignty or whether she lived in fear. Julie had strategies for helping women come to grips with the truth that God was up to good things because he is good. But Beth was not easily pegged.

Sometimes Beth appeared to be a world-weary cynic. She expressed disgust with her job, her family, her friends, and community leaders. She seemed to be apathetic about the world being a kind and good place. Julie's generation, the Boomers, had believed—really believed—that they could teach the world to sing in perfect harmony. Beth couldn't carry a tune and, sometimes, could barely mumble "whatever."

But at times Beth was almost giddy with anticipation about her own life. She held out great hope for her relationship with her boyfriend, Ben. She believed that she would succeed in her dream of being a graphic artist, in spite of the fact that she had been working at The Gap for eighteen months and was no closer to a career break than she had ever been.

To Julie, Beth seemed to be a crazy mix of optimism and pessimism. Her usual discipling strategies weren't working. She believed that she understood and could communicate the biblical concepts of God's goodness and how that leads to hope, but her words didn't seem to connect with Beth's heart. "I guess," Julie confided laughingly to a friend, "that Beth is just schizophrenic!"

Since We Gave Up Hope, We Feel a Lot Better

In fact Beth is a typical Xer when it comes to having hope. GenXers often have an odd heart mix of despair, indifference, and anticipation. Observers of our generation can't seem to agree if we are characterized by hope or hopelessness. Many have settled for a two-pronged description: Xers are hopeless about the world as a whole but hopeful about their own lives.

Is it really this simple? We suspect it is a bit more complex. When we get to know Xers beyond a surface level, it is clear that hopelessness is a powerful current in their lives, washing through both their inner and outer worlds.

Our generation has pretty much given up on the world as a whole. It is too polluted and decaying, and its leaders are too self-interested and corrupt. The best we can hope for is survival and for change on a small, local scale. We are a bit more optimistic about our own lives. Although the economy appears to be shrinking, we believe we will be able to find meaningful work and even prosper; 96 percent of us agree that "I am very sure that one day I will get to where I want to be in life."[1] Even though many of our families were broken, we are sure that our own marriages will last and that we will be close to our kids. We seem to have hope for our own lives.

Scratch the surface, though, and you see that what appears to be hope is actually little more than a determined effort to take our lives into our own hands. We plan on reaching our financial and vocational aspirations, not by playing the workplace game but by starting new enterprises, eschewing established businesses and mainstream companies. We want to have long-lasting marriages, but we are marrying less often and later in life. We are the "youngest copulating and oldest marrying generation ever recorded."[2] And nearly 30 percent of us live with our parents.

It is not that we are so hopeful, but that we think hard work and denial and even luck can mask our pain. We hope to be able to survive, to make it through another job, another relationship, another day with a minimum of damage in a world that is falling apart at the seams. This is not what the Bible calls hope.

Hope in a Hopeless World

"I'm looking for hope in a hopeless world," sings the band Widespread Panic, "I'm trying to find love in such hateful times." Real hope, the kind that gives us strength in the face of suffering, despair, and crumbling relationships, is elusive for Generation X, but it is the ace in the hole for followers of Christ.

This book is structured around the three cardinal Christian virtues—faith, hope, and love. Each is indispensable. But according to the New Testament, hope is foundational. In the introduction of his letter to the Colossian church, Paul expresses his gratitude to God because of the faith, hope, and love demonstrated in the lives of the Colossians. The faith and love evident in their lives, adds Paul, "spring from the hope that is stored up for you in heaven and that you have already heard about in the word of truth, the gospel that has come to you" (Col. 1:5–6). Hope evidently creates the climate in which the trusting confidence of faith and the outward expression of love can flourish.

Each of these three cardinal virtues points to a specific epoch of time. Love is rooted in the present and relates to the way we demonstrate the character of God in the here and now. Faith places its trust in God's promises, given credibility by his track record of faithfulness. And hope looks to the future, secure in the knowledge that the God who has proven himself worthy of our faith and has demonstrated his love in our lives will honor himself and those whom he loves. Hope is the settled confidence in the goodness of God and in his good sovereignty that enables us to face all of the circumstances of life with grace and courage and selflessness.

Without this settled confidence, we are "without hope and without God in the world" (Eph. 2:12). To be without hope is to be without God. When Douglas Coupland titled his novel *Life after God,* he was more on target than perhaps he even knew.

For Christian members of this "first generation raised without religion," hope begins with an ability to see what God is up to, to honestly see people and circumstances in our lives yet to believe that God is up to something good because he is good. We learn to trust that he will work things out for us because he loves us. And he will accomplish his good purposes in a way that brings life to those who love him and demonstrates his love, faithfulness, and mercy before all eyes.

This hopeful view of life does not come naturally to a generation that has a distinctively cynical take on the world and "actively pursues the deflation of the ideal."[3] This means that the stakes are high for those who disciple Xers. The prevailing story is laced with cynicism, pessimism, and hopelessness. Effective disciplers will help Xers to intersect with God's hopeful Story.

The Story of Hope

A key task of a discipler of Generation X is to help her disciple see her story in light of God's Story. The goal is a mature vision of the world that takes into account injustice, sin, and pain, without allowing these realities to dim our settled confidence in God's good oversight of our lives. The raw material for the Story is in God's track record in Scripture.

The Old Testament prophets and poets called the people of Israel again and again to *remember.* They were to remember God's faithfulness in the past, the ways in which he had proved himself strong and good and wise on behalf of those who loved him and whom he loved. Their corporate story was one of hope, of God's love and faithfulness against the odds and in the face of indifference and even rebellion.

In the same way, we can call GenXers to remember what God has done in their lives and in the lives of his corporate community. Remembering and reflecting on what we remember can create hope both for our lives and for the world.

Hope for My Life

In his more honest moments Ron wondered if he knew God at all. In the early days of being a Christian, God had seemed more real to him than any other person. He looked forward to getting up early in the morning to read his Bible and to pray, he found joy in sharing his faith with others, and he experienced a fulfillment he had never known. Dark areas of Ron's life—addictive habits, especially—gradually lost their power and he and others saw a noticeable softening in his heart for others, especially the materially poor.

Ron had been a Christian for five years now, and much of the early glow had worn off. While he still held to the convictions of his faith, much of his joyous spontaneity in spiritual disciplines was gone. A few of his old habits seemed to have regained some of their allure. He found himself growing angry more often than usual and struggling with sexual temptation.

Nearly desperate, Ron sought out his pastor, Steve. "I'm not even sure I'm a Christian anymore," he said through a clenched jaw. "I want to do the right thing, but it's such a struggle. I want to know God but I'm not sure if he wants to know me. I know I'm doing the wrong things and I want to stop but I'm unable to help myself."

It might not be Steve's first source, but he could find much help in the ministry of Jonathan Edwards, the New England pastor from the mid-1700s! Considered by many to be the finest theological mind America has yet produced, Edwards was first and foremost a pastor, intensely concerned with the hearts of his people.

The movement of God that has been called by historians the First Great Awakening got its impetus from Edwards's congregation in Northampton, Massachusetts. Characterized by a deep sense of personal sin and an attraction to Christ because of the beauty of his holy character, the revival spread throughout the New England states. Like all revivals, the Awakening had its share of abuses and its enemies, and Edwards quickly became a lightning rod.

Edwards had two sets of detractors. On the one hand were the conservative Boston clergy, some Unitarian, but others orthodox. They observed some of the emotional excesses of the revival in some churches and correctly surmised that the Awakening posed a threat to the status quo. They attacked Edwards and other revival leaders as "enthusiasts" bent on leading the common people astray.

On the other hand were the real enthusiasts, those who were fascinated with some of the more spectacular aspects of the revival and were rather bored with conviction of sin, repentance, and grace.

Caught between a rock and a hard place, Edwards turned to the activities he did best—thinking and writing. In response to the controversy, he produced one of the most penetrating studies of spiritual experience ever written, *Treatise on Religious Affections*.

Edwards's goal was simple—to set out the distinguishing marks of a work of God in the human heart and to contrast them with false or unreliable signs. He was concerned to prove that revival could happen while acknowledging that it could go bad.

"Affections" for Edwards are the core motivations of the heart, those things that determine everything we think, feel, and do. The affections shape and show who we are at bottom and they are manifested in our thoughts, emotions, and actions. Affections are more than emotions but they are very much involved with emotions.

Edwards began his discussion of the affections by listing a number of unreliable signs of God's working, including intense religious feelings, a certain sequence of affections, a physical display of religious affections, much or eloquent talk about God and religion, frequent and passionate praise of God, zealous or time-consuming devotion to religious activities, and being convinced that one has a good relationship with God.

Following this exposé, Edwards lovingly crafted a description of those reliable and true signs of God's grace working in the hearts of men and women. A true work of grace comes from a divine and supernatural source and is not humanly controlled. God is attractive for his own sake and for his beauty, not for what he can give us nor for what he saves us from. We are deeply aware of our sinfulness and our shortcomings and are sorry for them. As a result, we are humble. Over time, our very nature changes and our character looks more and more like Christ's. We develop a healthy fear of God that is not abject terror on one extreme or nonchalance on the other. Our lives are balanced between work and devotion, between reflection and experience, between thought and feeling. We have a consuming hunger for God, even if we do not pursue him perfectly. And our lives reflect the ethical and spiritual values of God's kingdom.[4]

What do these reflections of an eighteenth century minister have to do with Ron's life—and with ours? They can provide detail and color to those stories God is telling with our lives. The reliable signs of grace have appeared again and again as recurring motifs in the biblical Story as well as in the lives of followers of Christ who have lived since. To the extent that these qualities are apparent in our own life, we will know that we are living in the same story with other Christ-followers.

An adept discipler can help Ron and others like him examine the story of their lives in light of the New England story. If these reliable signs of grace are present in his or her life, we can assure a disciple that God is active and working in spite of personal failure, sin, and discouragement. If we know that God is up to something in our lives, we can learn to hope that this progressive work will change us into the people we long to be and that God wants us to be.

Narrative discipleship will link the biblical Story with the New England story and with my story. Each chapter of the story has a common thread—the work of God in our lives as his Story intersects and changes our own.

The affections are biblical and resonant and wise, to be sure. But their force for discipling may lie in the fact that they are drawn from and rooted in something solid, a part of the story that precedes but is linked to our own. If we disciple by using narrative from across the generations and even centuries, our discipling has the ring of something deep, true, tested, and real.

All the World's a Stage

Narrative discipleship takes into account drama as well as story. To the New England story, we can add the drama of Christian growth as seen by a converted slave-holder, John Newton.

Known mostly for his hymn "Amazing Grace," Newton was also quite a preacher, possessing a keen insight into spiritual psychology. In one of his most penetrating observations, Newton outlined the three issues or questions facing Christians as they grow and mature. For our purposes, we will call these the three acts of the Christian life.[5]

Act One: The New Christian

The key issue for new believers is *repentance*, learning to appropriate the gospel of grace on an ongoing, daily basis. New Christians face two chief temptations: to fall away when the newness of faith wears off and to become brash, judgmental, and disrespectful of those who have been Christians for a long time.

A discipler of a new Christian will practice patience and firmness and continually remind the one he is mentoring what it means to know God solely by God's grace.

Act Two: The Growing Christian

For the growing Christian, the key issue is *walking by faith,* especially when faced with suffering and disappointment. The Bible is clear that suffering and hardship are normative for Christ-followers. When a growing Christian encounters difficult times, he faces two primary temptations: to blame God or to blame himself. The first temptation undermines faith in God's goodness and is, in fact, an act of rebellion. The second temptation is less obvious but just as destructive in that it erodes intimacy with a loving Father.

It would be foolish to suggest formulaic responses for an issue as complex as suffering in the lives of Christians but it is important for a discipler to drive home two key truths: God is good and so everything that happens can be redemptive, and it is impossible for us to be punished for sins and failures because Christ has already taken our punishment in full. With a grounded understanding of God's good character and our own identity as adopted sons and daughters, we can face suffering and pain with honesty, integrity, and hope. We can struggle well with life.

Act Three: The Mature Christian

The key issue here is *communion with God.* Once the gospel has been rooted in our hearts and we have learned to follow God in the dark, we get to experience the riches of intimate communion with our Father. Tim Keller puts it delightfully: We realize in the end that the most important question concerns how to have a good quiet time.[6] Narrative disciplers who are working with maturing Christians will help their mentorees understand what it means to pray and meditate well, emphasizing such disciplines as *lectio divina* and using carefully some of the tools available for spiritual direction.

Using Newton's vision as a guide for spiritual growth, a narrative discipler can help the younger believer see his life as a drama, full of rich character development, twists and turns, challenges, romance, intrigue, and a rewarding and satisfying ending because of the craftsmanship of the Playwright.

Hope for My World

Christian hope is not limited to our own lives. And a hopeful Christian will grow to have a vision for how the hope of the gospel intersects with a hopeless world. The final task for a discipler seeking to inculcate hope into the life of an Xer is to help her see how micro-hope can extend to macro-hope. It is important that our generation understand that the gospel has relevance for all of life and that it can transform structures and institutions.

Generational theorists have suggested that Generation X will not have a lasting impact on the world in terms of positive change. The argument runs that we were dealt a bad hand and that we are survivors rather than heroes. We can look back to our Builder forebears and ahead to our Millennial heirs for inspiration, but they say the best we can expect is to struggle through.

Frankly, these generational theorists have ignored the God of hope. But our hope can be rooted in what God has done, is doing, and, most importantly, will do in history. Right now God is moving to sum up all things in Christ, to bring everything together under his lordship. History is headed toward a glorious, crashing climax when God makes everything new and wipes every tear from our eyes.

And in this in-between time, God gives us the privilege of joining in his mission with him. The mission is to be hope-bearers, to mimic God by putting things back together and living for reconciliation. We know that Christ has died in our place and so we have faith in God's promises and character. We have experienced Christ's forgiveness and so we can love without measure. And we are betting everything on his return and his promise to reintegrate everything that has been fragmented. Because of this, we can hope extravagantly. And through our life together in community, we can bring hope to hopeless people in a hopeless world.

PART 4

LOVE

Family Matters

The devil sees the potential work or power of a family for God. So he's concentrated much energy at tearing our family apart so that it doesn't become kinetic. And I must say that he has fought a worthy battle. But I believe God has never lost a battle.

Just a Coach in the Stands

It could have been the proudest day of Henry Bibby's life. He was being honored for the twenty-fifth anniversary of his team's NCAA basketball tournament victory. As point guard for the UCLA Bruins, Henry went on to lead his team to three consecutive tournament wins. On the anniversary of that day, twenty-five years later, he was on hand to watch his son Mike start as a freshman for the Arizona Wildcats in the championship game. It could have been the stuff of dreams.

Mike was a star in what was arguably one of the best championship games in the history of the NCAA men's basketball tournament. The Arizona Wildcats were matched up against Kentucky, the defending champions. The game was played with ferocious speed and strength by both teams, but in the end the young Arizona team's passion prevailed against powerful Kentucky in an overtime victory.

It was the first time a team had bumped off three number-one seeds—including our beloved North Carolina Tar Heels—to win the tournament. It was also the first time a freshman point guard had led his team to the tournament prize. Mike played with all the poise of an upperclassman as Henry watched from the stands.

After the game the two did not celebrate together, however. In fact they barely spoke to each other. Mike refused to talk about his famous father in interviews before or after the game. In the end, Henry Bibby was there as a coach and former player, not as Mike's father.

To understand the sad ending to this story, you have to go back many years. Henry had a family and a promising career as a coach until a recruiting scandal at Arizona State left him without a job. He hit the road without his family, taking coaching jobs in different states, even another country. Years passed and he never returned. Eventually his contact with Mike and his siblings was reduced to a pager number. Henry chose his career over his family. He won some games but lost his son.

The Changing Family

The Fatherless Family

Mike is an extraordinary talent but he is not unique among his peers. He is part of the generation with the most fatherless families in our history. In 1960 only 9 percent of families with children were single-parent families; by 1990 it was up to 27 percent and still climbing. A full 90 percent of those families are without dads.[1] One Xer told us, "My father left us when I was three. I thought it was normal. Neither of my best friends had a father either."

Many GenXers have lost a father or a mother to abandonment or divorce. The divorce rate continued to climb throughout their childhood and adolescence. In 1960 there were 393,000 divorces in the U.S. By 1980 the divorce rate had nearly tripled. Many studies have demonstrated that children of divorce are much more likely to have a deep sense of rejection and loneliness that often persists into adulthood. Judith Wallerstein, who has tracked the children of divorce for more than twenty-five years, finds strong evidence that the impact of divorce is long-lasting and cumulative. Of her sample of children of divorce, she found that 25 percent dropped out of high school, 40 percent had received psychological help, and 65 percent had poor relationships with their parents. They were twice as likely as their peers from intact homes to have these problems. In our own work and ministry, we see the awful legacy of divorce among Xers.

Even those with both parents together experienced unprecedented family stressors while growing up. They grew up hard and fast, letting themselves in by the latchkey, raising themselves on Pop Tarts, Atari, and Mister Rogers. Macaulay Culkin's prayer in the movie *Home Alone* sums up the endless hours without Mom and Dad: "Bless this highly nutritious microwave macaroni and cheese dinner and the people who sold it on sale. Amen." In 1987, 30 percent of junior high school and 38 percent of high school students were left to care for themselves after school "almost every day."[2] Usually there were no serious consequences. However, the lack of structure and supervision took its toll on some. One

133

Xer, now in his mid-twenties, told us that he had had nearly two dozen sexual partners and had a serious drug habit by the age of fifteen—without his parents' knowledge. Nearly all of his troubling behavior occurred from 3 P.M. to 7 P.M. By the time his parents drove up in the evening, he was alone in his room listening to his stereo. They never suspected a thing. His parents were together; they just weren't around.

The Floating Family

The disintegration of the family left an extraordinarily deep wound in this generation. Because of this, our generation's sense of what constitutes a family is still unclear. According to Barna, only 19 percent of GenXers define a family as a group of "individuals to whom you are closely related, by marriage or blood lines." However, 28 percent say a family is a group of "people with whom you have close relationships or deep personal/emotional bonds."[3] The family has now been termed "the floating family,"[4] because it is an ambiguously defined, ever-changing concept. Membership in the family is defined by the closeness of the relationships, not by marriage or birth or adoption.

"My friends *are* my family," said one GenXer, a 26-year-old graduate student. "I have stronger connections with them than I do with my own parents." Many in this generation express a similar sentiment. Author Elizabeth Wurtzel writes, "In fact, I think one of the many ways many of us twentysomethings have come to deal with our rootlessness has been by turning friends into family. . . . Of course, some pundits make fun of us for turning friends and ex-lovers into pseudo-family members, but I believe this is an arrangement that actually works."[5]

GenX minister Dieter Zander writes, "family is more frequently defined as those who will love them. Often, friends are more 'family' than are parents or siblings. Thus, community—open, safe, inclusive relationships in which people help each other rather than compete— is the highest value of this generation."[6]

With their dysfunctional and broken families, GenXers have sought to recreate a sense of kinship. They use their friends as brothers and sisters, aunts and uncles, even mothers and fathers. It may be an arrangement that actually works on one level, but on a deeper level, it may not work at all.

Not only do we have little consensus on what a family is, we have even less clarity on what is best for a family. Historically, most have agreed that a man and a woman married and living together with their children was the best arrangement. In the postmodern era, even that is called into question. As a culture, we no longer agree. The resulting disequilibrium has left GenXers to define family on their own terms.

The changing economic and cultural realities have changed many intact, traditionally structured families as well. Not long ago it was the norm for people to graduate from college and then move out on their own. This usually meant finding your own apartment, building a career, marrying, starting a family. For most people, all of this tended to happen by their middle or late twenties. Today the changing economic and social realities have caused many GenXers to move back home with their parents, even after graduating from college. One 26-year-old college graduate told us, "I'd love to move out. I just can't afford it." Consequently he sleeps in the same bedroom where he has lived since he was eleven.

Twenty-eight-year-old Joel Reese writes about having to move in with his parents. He says, "I keep asking myself: How could this happen? Don't I have a master's degree? And more importantly, aren't I out of high school? It's only a little comforting knowing I'm not the only one. A lot of college graduates my age are moving back home. They call us boomerang kids, or the excruciating ILYAS— Incompletely Launched Young Adults."[7] He goes on to reason that college tuitions have increased at twice the rate of inflation over the past twenty years, forcing nearly twenty-two million students to take out big student loans. Their debt, coupled with a tighter job market, comparably lower starting salaries, and more unpaid internships, often force Xers back home to live with their folks. This is the first generation since the Civil War whose standard of living does not equal or exceed that of their parents. These economic realities have changed the face of the family for many Xers. Compared to other generations, the GenXers' family looked different when they were kids; it still looks different now that they are adults. The shape of the family continues to change. The family is still floating.

The Frantic Family

Technology has changed the face of our culture forever. Less than a century ago most people spent their entire lives in the same community. Their towns consisted of familiar people with similar ways of thinking and living, and the cast of players in one's life drama was limited and stable. Geographical distance was a true barrier to developing relationships with people who lived outside of the local community.

With the advent of such things as the automobile, the radio, and the telegraph, the culture began to change. With the new technologies of the past thirty years our culture has become even more radically different. The world is abuzz with ever-new forms of technology—cell phones, computers, satellites, fax machines—that link us to more people in more parts of the world. We can regularly stay in touch with friends via e-mail and keep up-to-date with many people in different cities, different states, and different countries. When we need to travel to another state or country, we can do so quickly and with relative ease. When we return, we simply check our voice mail and e-mail to determine whom we should contact next.

The changes to our culture and our ministries brought about by technology have had both positive and negative impact. For example, when an overseas missionary who contracted a crippling disease was dying, his family instantly sent an e-mail to hundreds of people in several countries asking for prayer. When a friend found a new job and wanted people to celebrate with her, she sent out a group message to several people and got warm congratulations in reply and offers to help her find an apartment in her new city. When a church with a new leadership program for business professionals sent out announcements by fax to several corporate offices, it generated strong response and many young professionals showed up. These are undeniably good things.

These technologies have helped make us a socially saturated culture. We constantly communicate with others; we always seem to be busy interacting with people in one form or another. Consequently the expectations of business and family life have changed accordingly. We are people on the move, always driving and flying and dialing and faxing.

You have a new family reality: more kinetic, less connected. Even when families stay together, the members rarely join in the same routine anymore. Now we have an intermingling of multiple realities under one roof. Dad flies out of town on business once or twice a week. Mom has to get the youngest to daycare before work, pick up the middle child after school for piano lessons, catch the end of the oldest child's soccer game later. Dad drives himself home from the airport. At 8 P.M. when everyone is finally home, some have eaten; some haven't. The kids play and get ready for bed as the parents shuffle through the mail, listen to the messages on their answering machine, and check their e-mail. Even members of good, close families are whirled around each other by the tornado of postmodern life, and it's been this way since Xers were infants.

Adopted as Children

All of us understand our story in the context of our family, who raised us and shaped us. We are who we are in large part due to the influences—both positive and negative—of our family. For many GenXers, seeing that God is in control and up to something good is often hardest when related to family issues. When we talk with them about their family, we have to offer something beyond platitudes and pop psychology. We must offer them soul-changing truth. Our truth is that God is a good Father who has adopted us into his family. To know this in your soul is to be set free.

We both know something of the experience of adoption. Todd was adopted; Dave has adopted. For Christians, adoption is one of the greatest doctrines of the faith. We are adopted into the family of God. The Bible speaks of it in these terms only four times in the New Testament, yet the idea permeates the Scripture. J. I. Packer says adoption is "the highest privilege that the gospel offers."[8]

In theological terms, justification involves God in the role of judge, declaring believers righteous because of Jesus' sacrifice on the cross. But with adoption, God is in the role of father. Justification is a forensic term, a term of law; adoption is a family term. It refers to a love relationship between a father and his child. First John 3:1 says, "How great is the love the Father has lavished on us, that we should be called children of God! And that is what we are!"

The adopted sons and daughters of God have inherited an eternity of love. For believers, the best is yet to come. We look forward to the reality of heaven, knowing that it will be a homecoming—a family gathering—with God our Father surrounded by his beloved children. Christianity is a faith that looks forward. But even in the present, we live in the knowledge that we have a heavenly Father who loves us and cares for us. As with the kingdom itself, the fatherhood of God is both a present and future reality—one that we will not experience in all its fullness until heaven, yet one that changes us even now.

The Bible often speaks of the fatherhood of God. Over and over again, he is described as a good father. He is a proud father who makes a fuss over us. James 1:17 says, "Every good and perfect gift is from above, coming down from the Father of the heavenly lights, who does not change like shifting shadows." Many GenXers are well-acquainted with bad fathers, but God is different. He is a good father. He loves us, adopts us into his family, showers us with good gifts. Not only that, he remains faithful to us. He does not leave us as orphans. He does not change his affections toward us.

Understanding the fatherhood of God and our position as his adopted children is an important step for GenXers. In doing so, GenXers can move beyond the cognitive connection with God (i.e., God is a "storyteller" who has our stories firmly in hand) to an emotional connection with God. He has literally adopted us into his family and is a true father who loves, protects, nurtures, and cherishes us.

God our Father becomes our secure base. Out of his unwavering love, we are freed up to move boldly into other relationships, risking heartache and even rejection. We become free.

Free from Fear

A young boy named Joey had been horribly abused by his mother. He said, "When she was mad, she would kick me across the room." Sometimes she would lock him in his room or in the garage for hours at a time as punishment for crying. He was only three years old at the time. Finally a few years later, he was taken from his mother's custody and placed with an adoptive family. They loved him well and nurtured him, but he never bonded with them. He was always saying he wanted to go live with Teresa, his birth mother. His behavior became more and more disruptive in the home. He was destroying property, hurting the cat, punching and biting his siblings.

His adoptive parents asked him, "Why are you doing this?"

"I don't want to live here anymore," he said. "I want to live with Teresa again." He always referred to her by her first name.

"How do we treat you in this family?" they asked.

"Good," he said plainly.

"And how did Teresa treat you?"

"Bad," he said as plainly as before.

"What do you mean? What did she do to you?" they asked, hoping he'd remind himself of her mistreatment.

"She hit me."

"And what else?" they asked gently.

"And kicked me."

"And what else?"

"And didn't take care of me," he said without looking up.

"How did it feel to live with her?"

"It was scary," he replied.

"So where do you want to live?" they asked.

"With Teresa."

As incredible as this seems, it is a true story. The sadness of it is that even though this child has been rescued from a horrible life and brought into a wonderful family, he won't allow himself to be embraced by a loving family because of his early experiences. He is a prisoner of his early traumas. He is a slave to his fear.

In less dramatic ways, many GenXers are also slaves to their fears. Because of their early experiences, they are often insecure in their relationships, fearing negative evaluation and rejection. Often they desire intimacy yet fear it at the same time. Many cope by creating emotional distance. They become self-reliant. Yet God rescues them from this slavery to fear and self-reliance. The deeper realizations of our permanent adoption by God can transform our relationships with others. Paul writes, "For you have not received a spirit of slavery leading to fear again, but you have received a spirit of adoption as sons by which we cry out, 'Abba, Father!' The Spirit Himself bears witness with our spirit that we are children of God (Rom. 8:15–16 NASB). God's Spirit is a Spirit of adoption. His permanent seal on us chases away fear. We can live free of insecurity because we have a secure base. We can live free of self-reliance and trying to make our lives work by our own efforts.

With God as our Father, we also have new brothers and sisters. These spiritual siblings form our new community, a community of faith, hope, and love. It is in the context of this new community where most believers

141

first live out their freedom from fear. As brothers and sisters, we are called to pursue each other and to be pursued. It is here where we gently expose each other's fears so we can be fully known and still fully loved.

Free to Forgive

Understanding our adoption as sons and daughters of God allows us to forgive others, including family members, in ways that cut to our soul. We forgive deeply because we have been deeply, completely forgiven, and not only forgiven, but embraced and brought into an eternal family. The picture of God the Father in the parable of the prodigal son is of a dad who races out to hug his selfish, arrogant son and throw a party for him because he has returned home. Rose Miller writes, "The Father wishes for us to see the beauty of a life of forgiveness—of being forgiven by the Father and of ongoing forgiveness of others."[9] Her words are perfectly chosen. A life of forgiveness is a thing of beauty. To see it lived out in the lives of our generation moves us beyond words. A son's forgiveness of his dad's abandonment or a daughter's forgiveness of her mother's selfish control reflect God's model of love and forgiveness and flow out of a deep understanding of how much we have been forgiven by a Father who celebrates us.

Free to Fight for Others

When we experience the deep love of God for us, we become motivated to draw others into that love. We become partners with God our Father in the great fight for people's lives by praying for them. We pray for family members who don't know God and for those who act selfishly. One young GenXer named Brad had been abandoned by his father who literally ran off with the next-door neighbor. For years his dad made no attempts to contact the family. There were no calls at Christmas or on birthdays. Brad and his family boiled with hostility toward this selfish man. It wasn't until he began to pray for his dad that Brad felt released from his anger. He began to pray that his father's heart would be broken, that he would repent, that he would return to his family. The man has still not returned—at least not yet. But Brad has changed.

God takes great delight in bringing broken things back together, including broken relationships. He invites us into his family and from there he begins to mend our human families, but not always by bringing dads back home or changing selfish siblings—sometimes, but not always. But he does mend our own hearts and allows us to be free of fear, to forgive, and to pray.

Our family is part of us forever. Many of the scars that GenXers carry from their family experiences may never be fully healed this side of heaven. But God is powerful and active in our hearts and in our families.

This fatherless generation must know God as their Father. He redefines us as his children, and in doing so he calms our fragmented, frantic experience of family life. He frees us to move boldly into relationships with our earthly family. The realization that God is not only the one who tells our stories, but also acts in them as our good and loving Father is powerful indeed.

Please help me and my family Lord 'cause you're the only one who can.

Friends for Life

Boy, I'm really confused. I can't seem to find any real good friends up here. I thought I tried. I just can't seem to become a part of a group of good friends. I want that so badly. I'd do most anything to be in a place where people know me.

Woven into the Fabric of Our Lives

Have you ever seen a magnificent tapestry in a stately old mansion or church? Some hang more than twenty feet long and are adorned with pearls and threads of gold. The silk fabric is often brightly dyed, making stunning designs. Tapestries are beautiful masterpieces that often take months for artisans to create.

The Bible says that *we* are God's masterpieces (Eph. 2:10). Indeed, our lives are beautiful tapestries, each with a different design. The lives of others are woven into the fabric of our own. Some are short but vibrant threads; others are large colorful patches. Some dangle like tassels on the periphery, while others are an intricate part of our design. All help to make us the tapestry that we are.

The problem is that we see our tapestry from a limited perspective, as though we were viewing it from the underside. We see oddly formed shapes, threads that weave in and out and then disappear altogether, and no discernible pattern. God, however, is looking at our tapestry from up above. He sees the gorgeous design that he himself is weaving. To him, it is dazzling and magnificent. It is a work of art.

This image of a tapestry is a visual representation of the story of our lives. Like a tapestry, our story has many elements that come together to form a work of art. It's also like a play. The people who move in and out of our lives are all players. Some are bit players; others are there for support or comic relief; others take lead roles. All are important to the overall story. They give our story nuance, subtext, and structure.

The best plays, TV shows, and movies—whether they are dramas, comedies, or action-adventures—are built on solid characters and well-developed plots. The same is true for our stories. The good news is that each of us has a story that is being told by the master Storyteller. He is directing it and, with amazing precision, is able to weave it into the stories of others. This makes the characters richly colorful and the plot intricate and complex.

As we share with GenXers how God is at work directing the beautiful story of their life, we can show the interconnections of relationships and tell how God is taking ugliness and chaos and creating a work of art. From there we can help them take inventory of their relationships and distinguish true friends from acquaintances. Finally we can teach them how to be loyal truth tellers in their intimate friendships.

Term of Endearment, Term of Commitment

We've seen how GenXers often try to make their friends into family and, therefore, how the line between family and friends gets fuzzy. But problems with intimacy in family relationships are likely to translate to problems in friendships. Wayne Lockwood writes that he "got wrapped up in one of those youth groups, trying to replace a dysfunctional family with one that worked."[1] He abandoned the youth group and the Christian faith, trying one religion and philosophy after another. He writes that the whole notion of a "relationship" with God was a frightening concept for him. For GenXers, intimate relationships of any kind are often scary. And a tendency to run away from relationships when they become uncomfortable or uncertain will not be easily overcome.

In the Bible there are two words for friend. The first, *philos*, is a term of endearment. It is someone we like, someone we feel warm toward. The second word, *hetairos*, means a comrade. While there are many people to whom we are endeared, there are few we can count on to be true comrades, companions who walk with us through life. We believe that GenXers are most in need of comrades, friends who can move intimately through life with them.

With this in mind, consider two important dimensions of relationships: duration and depth. Some relationships are short-term. They last only a few years and are usually determined by geography. That is to say, your relationship continues only as long as you live close to the other person. Other relationships are long-term, spanning many years and phases of life. They tend to continue regardless of where one of the two of you may move.

The other dimension of a relationship is its depth. Some relationships are superficial. That is not necessarily bad; it is just a reality. These relationships may be enjoyable and fun but they lack true depth. The conversation is nearly always light; deeply personal issues are not shared. Other relationships are deep. The two individuals often share deeply from their hearts, making themselves vulnerable to each other.

147

Intersecting these two dimensions creates a grid that looks like this:

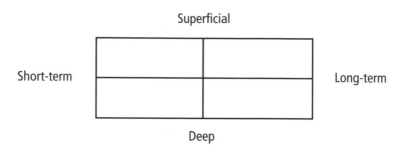

In the first box of the grid are those relationships that are short-term and superficial. We call these *acquaintances*. Most people have many acquaintances, some of whom they greatly enjoy. They may include relationships with classmates or coworkers. The interactions are pleasant but they tend to focus on superficial topics like sports, movies, or current events. These relationships are important because they expose us to many others who have a variety of interests, strengths, and perspectives. However, when one of the two individuals moves to a new city, the relationship is likely to end, except for chance meetings.

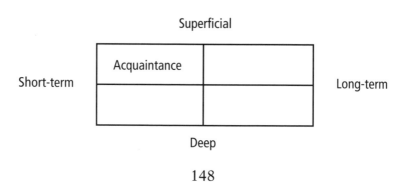

In the next box of the grid are those relationships that are superficial but may span a long period of time, through many phases of life. Often relationships that are begun in high school or college fit this description. The relationships begin superficially—as nearly all relationships do—but never become deeper. They may not deepen because the pattern of the relationship is difficult to change or because one of the individuals resists efforts to deepen the level of interaction.

Regardless of why they never deepen, many of our long-term relationships never graduate into intimate relationships. They are not necessarily bad relationships; in fact many of them may play important functions in our lives. They may be the relationships that serve as fun outlets for us. They are the people with whom we may go to ball games or shopping or for a weekend at the beach. The interactions are fun and rewarding but they lack depth and intimacy. A person with whom we have such a relationship could be called a *buddy*.

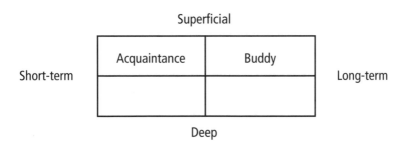

There are often many people in our lives that we know for only a short period of time, such as during our college years or while we live in a particular city. The relationships with those people may be deep; there may be a sense of real closeness and intimacy.

But once we move away, the relationship ends or fades away. There may be sporadic contact, but there is no sense of being meaningfully involved in each other's lives any longer. Such a person could be considered a *friend*.

These are important relationships that give us a glimpse of the lasting intimacy that we can enjoy in our relationship with God. For a brief season, we have a taste of true fellowship, true intimacy, and true joy in relationship with another person.

Superficial

Acquaintance	Buddy	
Friend		

Short-term   Long-term

Deep

All of these relationships have meaningful and good places in our lives, but the last category is perhaps the most important. These are the relationships that are not only deep and intimate, but also span over a large part of our lives. These are the individuals that seem to know us inside and out and stick with us, regardless of our faults. These relationships do not change regardless of circumstance or geography. These are comrades—the ones who are true brothers and sisters to us. We call these *life friends*. Most of us will only have a handful of individuals that we could consider true life friends; many people have no one that fits this description. These are our most meaningful and important relationships.

Superficial

Acquaintance	Buddy
Friend	Life Friend

Short-term   Long-term

Deep

The reason we delineate relationships in this way is that it allows us to take stock of our friendships. We can see that not all of our relationships qualify as friendships and even fewer are likely to become life friends. Such an understanding can allow us to move into relationships with more purpose and direction. Each of us can think of the people in our life with whom we could be life friends and we can become more intentional in our relationships.

This understanding alone does not necessarily yield healthy or deep relationships. For GenXers the desire to be close to others is strong, but there has been much damage in their ability to be intimate. They need direction in how to relate to others in deeper ways.

Undoing the Damage

Evan is a twenty-four-year-old man who became a Christian his junior year in college. His relationship with God has had its ups and downs, but he hangs in there despite his anger and doubts. His relationships with others are even more troubled at times. He can be as demanding and petulant as a child. He wants to do better but he doesn't know how.

While growing up, he was berated by his father, an alcoholic who would often hit his wife in front of Evan and his sister. Evan swore to himself that he would never hit a woman but in recent years he has gotten dangerously close. Last month he pinned his girlfriend against the wall during an argument. He spent the rest of the evening crying inconsolably. Despite his strong desire to change and his resolutions to shape up, he continues to struggle deeply in his relationships.

It is a sad fact that most of us grow up to replicate the style of relating that was modeled for us when we were young. Those who suffer abuse often become abusers as adults, even though determined to be different. This goes against logic, but it is not a logical process. As believers we can hold out a real hope for change, but it may come slowly, with numerous setbacks.

Many members of GenX—even those who have not been abused—have had poor role models for relationships. Often their role models have abandoned their commitments and acted selfishly. This is likely to translate to more of the same in GenXers' relationships.

The role of a discipler, then, is both to model healthy ways of relating and to teach what it means to be a good friend. GenXers must learn that two critically important characteristics of a good friend are loyalty and truthfulness.

Loyalty

For most of us, a relationship typically unfolds in a predictable way. We intersect the life of another person whom we find interesting and attractive in some way. We may have similar interests or senses of humor. We find ourselves spending more time with him. As we begin to know the person better, we may develop a fonder appreciation of him but we also see more of his irritating habits and the rough edges of his personality.

The fiery temper that was not evident before often flares up, the sarcastic comments become more cutting, or his opinions begin to annoy us.

It is at this point that we can fade out of the relationship or persist through it. To be honest, there is often just cause to fade out of a relationship early on. We are not obliged to pursue a deep relationship with every acquaintance. But there are true friendships from which we should not quickly retreat just because they become difficult. Every relationship is likely to frustrate and disappoint us at some time, but it's often the perseverance in hard times that helps a healthy, mature relationship to develop.

There will be times when a friend not only irritates you, but disappoints you in a significant way. She wrongs you in a blatantly selfish way. She betrays your trust and hurts you deeply. When it would be easier to let the relationship slip away, it takes both courage and hard work to persevere. It is hard not to end difficult friendships, but one of the marks of a Christian is demonstrating loyalty in relationships.

When discipling GenXers, it is vitally important to exhort them to remain loyal to their significant friendships, even when those relationships become difficult or painful. As a mentor, help the younger believer fight against the tendency to neglect or slip out from hard relationships. Challenge your disciple to remain loyal in friendship.

Truthfulness

It was Lisa's twenty-second birthday party and a dozen of her friends were there. One of them, Dominic, was talking loudly and gesturing wildly. Later that evening, one of his closer friends caught up with him in

153

the kitchen and whispered, "You are trying way too hard. You don't always have to be the center of attention." His face became red. His first instinct was to become defensive, but instead he said nothing. He was quiet the rest of the evening. He thought about the comment for days afterward. In later gatherings, he found himself examining his motives and working hard not to be selfish with attention. The words from his friend were sharp and they punctured his pride but they caused him to look at himself more closely and begin to change.

There is a great verse in Proverbs that says, "Wounds from a friend can be trusted" (Prov. 27:6). When a true friend says something painful, we can trust that the "wound" that is inflicted is for our growth. It may hurt for now but it will make us stronger in the long run.

Hard words can build us up or tear us down. The key is whether these words come from a loyal friend who has the motive to build us up. Someone we believe to be committed to us can speak tough words that help us grow and mature. They provide us with much needed feedback about our behavior, our words, and our motives. We may resent them initially, but in months or years to come, we may appreciate the marks that they have left on us.

A person earns the right to say hard things by being a loyal friend. Often it takes years to earn this right; it is no small matter. Many of us have met other Christians who believe that they are somehow entitled to say harsh things to others, even without a firm base of relationship or understanding with the other person. Make no mistake: Being a Christian does not give anyone license to be a jerk. And frankly, many harsh Christians are pious jerks.

With this said, however, many more Christians fail to speak the truth to their friends. They watch passively as their friends make grave mistakes or fall into grievous sin. They may do even worse. They may say nothing to their needy friend, yet talk at length with others behind his back. They figure his life out for him, map out his motives, and determine his decisions, all without ever breathing a word of it to him.

This, of course, is much easier and much more exciting than getting involved in the messy business of saying hard things and risk upsetting our friends. It is easier to let the friend make her blunders while hiding behind the oft quoted, "I can't make her decisions for her."

A loyal friend not only earns the right to say a tough thing, but often has the responsibility to say it. Our responsibility is to speak truth when it can help our friends mature or steer clear of sin. As friends, we speak truth even when it is tough to do.

To mentor a GenXer in the area of friendships, move from the big-picture understanding of what God is doing in our lives—telling a story—to an understanding of the different types of relationships. Challenge him to develop and nurture at least one life friend. Finally, model and teach what it means to be loyal in friendship and why it is important to speak the truth in love.

Someone like Evan will only mature and change in the context of relationships with friends who are loyal truth tellers. He is a hard person to love. His problems in relationships are tenacious, but there is hope for him. God will be loyal to him. God will be truthful to him. God will love him. Hopefully others will too.

GenX Sex
By Ellen Verhaagen

I'll state my goal now: to find a woman who I can love and care for, one that will complete the other half of my puzzle. How much more beautiful that picture will be when the perfect pieces of a woman chosen by my Lord are placed in the puzzle and matched to form one image of caring and love and devotion.

"I Want Your Sex"

A classic television ad, sponsored by Partnership for a Drug-Free America, shows an overhead camera close-up of a frying pan heating a pat of butter. The narrator's voice booms, "This is your brain." An egg cracks open and drops into the sizzling grease, and the narrator adds, "This is your brain on drugs." As we watch the egg cook, we hear, "Get the picture?"

This image of "frying your brain" clearly illustrates the consequences of drug use. The media presents a unified front against drugs and the resulting effects of drug use but they give mixed messages about the subject of sex. Soap operas, sitcoms, and especially advertisements all use sex as enticement to watch and to buy, while at the same time, there are ad campaigns geared to educate us about teen pregnancy and the horror of AIDS. In 1994 the Alan Guttmacher Institute issued a report titled "Sex and America's Teenagers," which included some eye-opening statistics. Teen sex is on the rise. Fifty-six percent of young women and 73 percent of young men today have had intercourse by age eighteen, compared with 35 percent of young women and 55 percent of young men in the early 1970s. Three million teenagers—about 1 in 4 sexually experienced teens—acquire a sexually transmitted disease every single year.[1] And yet youth's innate sense of invincibility is apparent when their overwhelming sentiment is "Well, I'm sure that won't happen to *me!*"

God knew what he was doing when he set sex apart, reserved only for marriage. His reasons need to be presented to this generation in a way that makes sense, perhaps wrapped around an image as powerful as a frying egg.

How God Sees Sex

Sex is a sacred, holy thing, set apart to be experienced in a loving, committed relationship between husband and wife. It is not dirty; it is a beautiful thing. Read any part of the Song of Solomon in the Bible to see the eloquent language used to describe the lover and his bride. It is only the misuse of sex that makes it ugly. It is an amazing fact that God invented sex. He thought it up!

In Genesis 2:20–25 we witness the unfolding of marriage and sex as God's idea for his human creation.

But for Adam no suitable helper was found. So the LORD God caused the man to fall into a deep sleep; and while he was sleeping, he took one of the man's ribs and closed up the place with flesh. Then the LORD God made a woman from the rib he had taken out of the man, and he brought her to the man. The man said,

"This is now bone of my bones and flesh of my flesh; she shall be called 'woman,' for she was taken out of man."

For this reason a man will leave his father and mother and be united to his wife, and they will become one flesh.
    The man and his wife were both naked, and they felt no shame.

Sexual intercourse was never intended to be a casual act. As defined in the passage above, a man leaves his mom and dad to create a new family in joining with his wife. "Becoming one flesh" is inherent in the definition of sex; two people who are sexually active are no longer two separate people. They have given up parts of themselves to become united, one flesh.

Sex is meant to be the culmination of the process of becoming naked with one other person, specifically your spouse. But the more I talk to GenXers, the more I realize nakedness is a common occurrence in dating relationships. In the words of James, "My brothers, this should not be." (James 3:10). The Bible attributes a lot of significance to nakedness. Check out the last verse in the passage above: "The man and his wife were both naked, and they felt no shame." I will put forth a corollary: If a man is with a woman who is not his wife and they are both naked, it is shameful. Many times Scripture links nakedness and shame—but not for the married. Marriage is a covenant relationship where two people, a man and a woman, become one. Isaiah explores this more in Isaiah 57:8: "Behind your doors and your doorposts you have put your pagan symbols. Forsaking me, you uncovered your bed, you climbed into it and opened it wide; you made a pact with those whose beds you love, and you looked on their nakedness."

In the context of this chapter, Isaiah is referring to idol worship and using an adultery analogy. The Israelites had left their husband and maker, God, and had taken other lovers. And it's obvious in this verse that opening your bed wide, making a pact with other lovers and looking on their nakedness, is not what God wants from his children.

In Ezekiel 16:32–38, Jerusalem was compared to an adulterous wife. "This is what the Sovereign LORD says: Because you poured out your wealth and exposed your nakedness in your promiscuity with your lovers, and because of all your detestable idols. . . . I will bring upon you the blood vengeance of my wrath and jealous anger" (Ezek. 16:36, 38).

Here the Lord says that exposing your nakedness in promiscuity with other lovers is one of several things that incur his wrath and jealous anger. So I say to this generation: "Don't be gettin' naked with each other!" It is not what God wants people to experience outside the context of marriage.

The engagement period is the time when you increasingly become more emotionally, intellectually, and spiritually "naked" or vulnerable with your fiancé, and sex on your wedding night is the last part of the process—the time when you become physically naked with each other. This event is so special and so powerful, God has set it apart, intending it to be experienced only between partners for life. He has "fenced it off" with a loving boundary.

Loving Boundaries

Let me illustrate it this way: A father and his toddler are playing in the living room. Then, wanting to be a good father, he takes the child upstairs and says, "I love you. I want you to have the freedom and independence that you desire. I want you to truly enjoy life by making your own choices. Now, go play!" Is that dad really showing love for his child by not mentioning the danger of the stairs? Shouldn't he, in the best interest of the child, latch a gate at the top of the stairs to prevent the child from falling down?

That's in effect what God had done in "fencing off" sexual intercourse to be experienced only within the commitment of marriage. That boundary has been set for our welfare by one who knows what's best for us.

Back to my analogy: As soon as the father latches that gate, what does the baby try to do? He tries to climb over the gate, break the boundary, step over the line, get as close to the edge as he can. And we try to do the same thing. We don't like boundaries. We don't like limits. Why? Because we are all sinners living in this world. If "sin" means doing what you please with no boundaries—going on a pleasure hunt with no limits placed on our sexuality—then as sinners we are going to try to bend the rules and break away from the authority God has over our lives.

This generation understands, probably better than any previous generation, the effects of people's natural inclination to go beyond boundaries with no regard for the consequences. Environmentally GenXers have rallied behind causes like the preservation of rain forests and saving the ozone layer. Relationally they have experienced the painful consequences of a skyrocketing divorce rate and an increase in child abuse—all because generations before them overstepped boundaries. The world is screaming, "NO LIMITS. COMPLETE FREEDOM. NO BOUNDARIES. NO CONSEQUENCES." But what I believe this generation needs to hear is this: God gives loving boundaries *and* choices with consequences.

Choices with Consequences

When two people come together in the act of sex, it's like taking two pieces of construction paper—one red and the other blue—swiping both with an Elmer's Glue Stick, and pressing them together. Sex bonds two people together, cementing the relationship. But if that act was casual or noncommittal and you break up and break apart, those two pieces of paper *that are now one* have to be torn apart. The blue has bits and pieces of red stuck to it; the red has torn strips of blue adhered to it. And if that happens continually with different partners over time, your construction paper is covered with ragged bits of many colors; it is torn, rough, and ugly.

After having spoken about this illustration to a group of college women, one approached me in tears. She said, "I've got torn construction paper on my soul! It hurts so bad that I gave part of myself away. Is there any way I can be a clean sheet again?"

Jesus came to earth to make us clean sheets again, to piece back our relationship to God the Father, which was torn apart by our sin. He can do the same with our torn-up construction paper; he can piece it back together again. I believe that many of the emotional scars will remain from our choices to have sex before marriage. However, in God's mind, when we repent, the slate is wiped clean; the page becomes one solid color again. We cannot physically become a virgin again but we can *spiritually* become a virgin as we ask God to forgive us for making wrong choices. There is substantial healing in his loving touch.

God's intention, when two people have sex, is that they are bonded together, never to come apart. His boundary of sex being "fenced off" for marriage has a loving reason behind it; he wants us to enjoy the pleasures of one man, one woman, together forever—a clean, pure, committed, increasingly cemented, and strong love.

There are many negative consequences to sex outside of marriage that can be articulated in the context of the discipling relationship.

Guilt

After speaking to a large group of college students on the subject of sex, a girl hung around to talk to me about her situation. Her dad was on the staff of a youth ministry, she grew up in a Christian home, and she'd accepted Christ at an early age. However, she told me that no one had ever clearly explained to her *why* it was God's intention for her to remain celibate until marriage; her parents had just said, "Don't do it!" She had slept with her boyfriend throughout their two-year relationship, and after they broke up she felt the pain of having given herself away. She told me of the incredible feelings of guilt that had weighed on her after they slept together the first time and how those feelings got less and less intense as time passed. Soon she had totally rationalized their passion by saying God wouldn't have given them overwhelming sexual attraction for each other unless he thought it was good and right.

God sometimes uses our feelings of guilt to make us aware of wrongdoing and to lead us back to him. So we must not ignore the voice of our guilt.

163

Blocked Communication

As a relationship becomes more and more familiar with regard to the physical expression of love, it becomes so easy to rely on touch rather than words for communication. If I kiss a man and he kisses me back, there is immediate gratification and no need for words. If I speak to a man and he speaks to me, communication occurs only when he hears my words, listening to the emotions and motives behind them, and then forms his response according to his own experiential grid. The latter communication is much more complicated. So if either partner in a nonmarital sexual relationship is tired or stressed or upset or bored, there is no real motivation to go the rougher road of verbally hammering through these emotions. Instead it is simpler to use sex as a way to deflect intense discussions and receive an immediate release and reward. One woman told me that after she broke up with her boyfriend, they saw each other at a party. Suddenly she realized they had absolutely nothing to talk about. Even though sex had been a regular part of their relationship, they were not really ever friends. For them, sex had taken center stage and had left no place for other important forms of communication.

One girl told me that after she consented to sex with her boyfriend, they stopped planning their date nights. Instead, they both became consumed with "Where are we going to do it next? When are we going to do it next? How are we going to do it next?" In relationships where sex becomes the myopic focus, other aspects of the relationship atrophy. Communication between two people in a relationship occurs not only through physical touch, but through words during a lively discussion, in serving our partner by helping with chores, and by spending quality time together doing nothing. This type of communication moves the relationship to a deeper—even more intimate—level than the stunted growth that occurs from a sexual focus.

Insecurity

When a relationship is built on little more than sexual attraction, feelings of inadequacy and jealousy are likely to occur when changes in one partner affect their sexual relationship. After two or three weeks of no sex, K. C. Boyles writes about his frustrating thoughts about his partner:

> But maybe I should just relax. Things happen, things stop happening—it sort of comes and goes with the tides, except maybe more mysteriously. We're a little bored with us right now, but we'll come around. Just relax, try to understand that this is the dynamic of the relationship at the moment, and that's okay. . . . [But] it's not all innocent suspicion. There's this other, toxic voice that says that she'd be having plenty of sex if she were with somebody else. This kind of generalized jealousy is poison. It says that you're not man enough for her, that you don't satisfy her; it says she's not the person she's pretending to be. This is a door I don't want to open—it's a little too hard to get it shut again, after a few nights of staring at the ceiling.[2]

Memories and Comparison

A friend of mine was "wild" in his younger days and he slept with a lot of women. As a Christian single during the last ten years, he has struggled to remain celibate. He told me he envies the privilege I had of being a virgin when I married, because he would always carry with him the memories of all his previous partners and I would remember only one—my husband. He is afraid that he will compare his wife-to-be to the best sexual partners of his past. He knows doing this won't be very honoring to her and he is worried that he'll inadvertently communicate that she doesn't measure up to his past experiences.

Your Relationship with God

There was a *20/20* special where teens were given free rein with video cameras. Their task was to interview friends about sex. One teenage girl said an interesting thing. She said she looked all over the Bible for any reasons not to have premarital sex and couldn't find any. I can find lots. The Bible uses the word "fornication" (in the King James version) or the words "sexual immorality" (in the New International Version) to mean anything that occurs sexually between two people outside of marriage. "But among you there must not be even a hint of sexual immorality, or of any kind of impurity, or of greed, because these are improper for God's holy people" (Eph. 5:3).

So many young people have strayed from faith and fellowship because their active sex life produces a barrier between them and God. That barrier could be produced by any sin, but sexual sin has a more weighty feel. One girl said she felt like such a hypocrite both in her church and in her home because she was sleeping with her boyfriend. We prayed together for God's forgiveness and she repented of her sexual past. She said she now looks forward to reigniting her passion for God.

How Sex Fits into the Story

There is a very positive abstinence movement among GenXers today that supports the idea that it is cool to wait until marriage to have sex. The Christian community needs to come alongside and concurrently present solid biblical reasons to wait as well.

In narrative discipling, we understand that sex is part of God's story. He began with Adam and Eve, calling them to "leave and cleave" (Gen. 2:24). After the flood, his command to Noah's sons and his sons' wives was, "Be fruitful and increase in number and fill the earth" (Gen. 9:1). Sex is part of the story that God is telling. But it is important to communicate that when God encourages sex, it is always within the loving boundary of marriage. What single GenXers need to hear is this: There are negative consequences to sex outside of marriage and there are rewards for celibacy. The rewards include but are not limited to: zero memories of past lovers—only enjoyment of your spouse alone, freedom of sexual expression without shame, and a truer understanding of holiness in being set apart by God. More important, GenXers need to hear God's loving intent and design for sex. The God of the universe desires for his people to see sex as he created it—as a gluestick for marriage.

Ellen Verhaagen is Dave's wife, Christy and Abbey's mom, and a former staff worker with InterVarsity Christian Fellowship. She is a frequent speaker on college campuses.

PART 5

THE HOPEFUL COMMUNITY

Building Community

I have joined this sweeping force of people who believe in our God. I have a calling and, although I don't know specifics, I know where it's heading and it's exciting.

Subcontracting for Community

Can you imagine what it would be like for everyone in the world to speak the same language? For one brief moment, near the dawn of human history, everyone did. At that time people lived a nomadic life, moving eastward across the plains, wanderers looking for a home. It is a hard thing to be homeless. Life is difficult as a nomad. So the people were looking to find security, a place to belong. They were looking to create community.

At first glance, creating community seemed to be an easy proposition for these desert wanderers. After all, there was no "them." There was only "us." And they were all alike, sharing a common culture and a common tongue. But attempts to create community have a way of becoming institutionalized—sometimes in utopian social structures, sometimes in literal structures.

The wanderers turned to each other and said, "Hey, let's make some bricks and build a great tower." Fired by their enthusiasm, the leaders among them wanted to push the envelope. "Let's build a huge tower, one that reaches all the way to the heavens and a great city will spring up around it. We'll make a name for ourselves. We'll be famous and respected. We'll be secure. Our community will be safe, and we won't be scattered if we can build this monument to ourselves."

According to the ancient writer, God looked down in disdain and mocked the wanderers. "Oh, no," he said, tongue in cheek, "if all of these wanderers speaking the same language succeed in building this city and this tower, there will be no stopping them! They might even take my place!"

And so God came down and scattered the wanderers, confusing their language, destroying their ability to communicate, and shattering any pretense at self-sufficient community building (see Genesis 11).

Community Happens? Not!

The story of the Tower of Babel is repeated every time humans try to build community from their own resources. The problem with self-made community is that it always comes from insecurity at the best, and arrogance at the worst. Self-made community, without reference to God, is self-serving and self-protective. Such attempts always collapse under their own weight. You can't sustain community, which requires great artistry and delicate balance, on a foundation of pride or fearful need.

No generation in recent memory has valued relationships more than ours. Many of us are from broken homes, so talk of our friends being like family is not sentimental, idle chatter. Such talk reflects our heart hunger to connect, to experience belonging and community. The great irony is that we are less well equipped to connect and live in community than almost any other generation.

People learn how to relate to others in our families of origin. From our earliest days, we learn how to treat others and how we can expect to be treated in return. Theoretically the family is the place where we learn about mutual support, acceptance, and compassion. We learn to sacrifice for others and to meet another's needs, to value someone else's welfare more than our own. This is the way it is supposed to be.

The story of our generation, however, is that many of our families were not this way. We came of age in a time where children were less valued than they are now or they were previously. We long to be in community and to have meaningful relationships, but we are not equipped to do so.

Dineh Mohajer is an Xer who happens to be a wealthy, entrepreneurial small business owner in California. "I function like an average human being of my age," she says. "I go to clubs and movies and watch MTV. It's so *fun*. I'm a TV junkie. I need to go to Melrose Anonymous! Eating Cap'n Crunch and watching TV—two things I live for. Twice a week we have all-girls' night. My best friends come over. We watch TV and gossip and scream and yell and do our nails."[1]

Fun for a night, perhaps. But not when this is what you live for. And not when this is the depth of your relationships.

The Tale of Another City

They devoted themselves to the apostles' teaching and to the fellowship, to the breaking of bread and to prayer.

173

Everyone was filled with awe, and many wonders and miraculous signs were done by the apostles. All the believers were together and had everything in common. Selling their possessions and goods, they gave to anyone as he had need. Every day they continued to meet together in the temple courts. They broke bread in their homes and ate together with glad and sincere hearts, praising God and enjoying the favor of all the people. And the Lord added to their number daily those who were being saved.

Acts 2:42–47

Often we ask audiences to whom we are speaking "What was the bottom-line reason why Jesus Christ came to earth?" The answers are fairly predictable: "To be our example." "To die for our sins." "To provide for our salvation." The instinctive response for most evangelicals relates to personal salvation; Jesus came so that individual people could be reconciled to him by faith.

This is true as far as it goes. But it is not a complete answer. The Bible speaks surprisingly little of individual salvation, because it speaks relatively little of individuals. The writers and original readers of the books of the Bible were much more likely to think of themselves as members of a community, a covenant community to be more precise.

From its opening pages, the Bible portrays God as one who makes and keeps covenants with his corporate people. God deals with individuals, to be sure, but these individuals are usually cast as representatives of the covenant community. The fundamental object of salvation in the Old Testament is Israel, not Israelites. In the New Testament, the recipient of grace is usually the church, not individual Christians.

The primary reason Jesus came, we tell our audiences, was to prepare for himself a new covenant community,

174

which will be his bride. He came to form the church. His great purpose is to create a new community made up of those who have encountered his grace and who commit to living out the results of that encounter together.

God intends for men and women to live together in a community centered on the forgiveness he gives us in grace. The community is to be characterized by forgiveness, love, and hope. It is to be a new community of hope.

Thousands of years after God had scattered the wandering nomads, another group gathered together. This group was diverse in ethnicity, unlike the nomads. But like the nomads, God visited them and caused them to speak in other tongues (see Acts 2:4–21). In this case, though, the proliferation of language was a uniting rather than a dividing force. God the Spirit came in power and brought unity in the midst of diversity. He gathered people together rather than scattering them.

This new community of pilgrims was brought together by the shattering events of Passion Week, namely the arrest, trial, execution, and resurrection of Jesus Christ. Stunned by shock, sadness, and then grace, they gathered together in one place. They were at a loss. "You know you come with empty hands, or you don't come at all," writes the songwriter Bill Mallonee, and this was an empty-handed group, armed only with a desperate, reckless hope.

They were as unlike the early wandering nomads as they could be. Far from a self-serving attempt to carve our personal significance and force a secure community, these pilgrims knew that they could live only if God showed up and did something. He did. He formed a new community.

After God the Spirit came in power, one of their number, Peter, stood and proclaimed the central truth of the universe: Jesus, the God-Man, has been crucified for our sins but he arose from the dead because death could not defeat him. Consequently he offers us forgiveness, reconciliation, and full life. Thousands responded, were drawn together, and the first branch of the new community took shape (see Acts 2:14–41).

They devoted themselves to knowing and following the essential truths about Jesus. They shared a common life together, including joy and suffering, giving and receiving. They met one another's needs, even financial ones. They were generous and gracious and hospitable. They worshiped God together, and witnessed him do amazing works of healing and restoration. They shared communion together, centering the rhythms of their community around commemorating the cross. They prayed together and shared communion with God. They spent much time together, much time.

And others were drawn to them, irresistibly. Awed by the quality of life in the new community, they left their old lives, swore off old allegiances, and gambled everything on the Man so recently executed as a common criminal.

The nomads of Babel were self-sufficient, arrogant, fearful, self-centered, and disintegrating. The pilgrims of Jerusalem were interdependent, humble, joyful, God-centered, and multiplying. The nomads of Babel craved and tried desperately to structure security. The pilgrims of Jerusalem lived out of a secure center. The people of Babel were masters of agenda creating. Those of Jerusalem cared only for God's agenda, his larger purpose. The people of Babel were scattered and alone. The people of Jerusalem were gathered into community.[2]

Awesome Community

Our generation craves community but has no idea how to find it. This stark fact is a source of great hope for followers of Christ, who long to disciple Generation X. God is about forming his new community. Xers can give up their attempts at self-protective pseudocommunity and be a part of the awesome thing God is doing.

GenX leader Sean Meade speaks often of "awesome community" as being the most effective apologetic for our generation. The quality of the Jerusalem community inspired awe in "everyone" and led countless numbers to become a part of what God was doing (see Acts 2:43). We have a keen ability as a generation to sniff out cant and hype. We don't want anything less than the real deal. God's new community, in all of its current imperfection, is the real deal because it is God's deal.

God is telling a Story through his new community. It is a story of broken people moving toward wholeness, of sinful people moving together toward holiness, of marginalized people finding acceptance, and of lonely people finding family. It is a place where gifted people use their gifts to serve others, wealthy people use their resources to meet others' needs, and talented people use their talents for God and others without facing the envy and competition to which they are accustomed.

All of the discipling of Xers that we will do will head to this end: to help our friend see her story intersect with God's Story and then link up with the stories of others in community.

This means that we will pray for and work for authentic communities of faith. This means that we will root out, bring to light, and confess self-protective and self-serving patterns in our lives and churches, patterns that militate against community. It means that we will open our homes and lives and wallets to those in need. And it means that we will confront the postmodern, distinctively American god of individualism and self-interest head-on with the gospel, which tells us that we find ourselves only when our self is lost.

The account of the Jerusalem community is not a recipe or blueprint for community. There is a sort of evangelical utopianism that suggests, "If only we could get back to the purity of the early church, things would be perfect." As the New Testament letters reveal, those early Christians were anything but ideal, living with all the lusts and misdirection and selfishness that we do! But the Jerusalem community, if only for a time, tasted sweet wine. The message of Acts 2 is that these are the sort of things God does when he gets to call the shots and do his work of community building. This is a community of hope.

The New City

> Then I saw a new heaven and a new earth, for the first heaven and the first earth had passed away, and there was no longer any sea. I saw the Holy City, the new Jerusalem, coming down out of heaven from God, prepared as a bride beautifully dressed for her husband. And I heard a loud voice from the throne saying, "Now the dwelling of God is with men, and he will live with them. They will be his people, and God himself will be with them and be their God. He will wipe every tear from their eyes. There will be no more death or mourning or crying or pain, for the old order of things has passed away."
>
> He who was seated on the throne said, "I am making everything new!"
>
> Revelation 21:1–5

Discipling Generation X is a thrilling, daunting, impossible task. It will require every ounce of energy and passion and skill and patience we have. We will succeed because God requires it.

The third city, the new Jerusalem, is the end of the Story God is telling. The climactic chapter is breathtaking, tender, and too good not to be true. God is fundamentally about summing up all things in Christ, about putting broken things back together again. He is about bringing reconciliation and peace. In the new city, we will see the final results of his handiwork and the culmination of our hopes and dreams. Those of us who have committed ourselves to following Christ and discipling Generation X will see together what God has been up to all along, and it will be beyond our wildest dreams.

We are seeing the early signs of this now, as God stirs the hearts of more and more Xers to follow him for the first time or to follow him with greater purpose. The first generation raised without religion is becoming a generation after God.

AN EVENING AT CARIBOU

Party of Five

Two things about our generation: We like to hang out and we like good coffee. With this in mind, we chose Caribou, a popular coffeehouse in Charlotte, as the place to hang out and talk about discipling Generation X with a roundtable of Xers.

We wanted to test if the ideas we have developed in this book apply to real life, if they are meaningful to Xers who are being discipled and are themselves discipling others. We developed the narrative discipling model by doing hands-on ministry, discipling Xers, and learning as we went. However, narrative discipling as a distinct, coherent approach—with a name—is new. We wanted to test it out on a jury of our peers.

And so we chose a panel of five Xers to discuss the issues raised by this book. All of them are in their early to mid-twenties and are Christians. All are viewed by their peers as spiritual leaders. All are involved in a local church and other ministries. Most important for our purposes, each has been discipled and mentored by another and is currently discipling or mentoring someone else in turn.

This was our panel:

Michael has followed his father into business as a CPA. You would never know it to meet him, though, because Michael is a classic extrovert. He is winsome, charming, devout, and has a remarkable gift of evangelism. He quickly and easily wins the trust and respect of others. He also thinks deeply and honestly about his faith.

Phil has the most interesting educational pedigree of our panel: a double major in mathematics and Russian from Duke. Phil is working currently at a bookstore as he weighs future career options, which may include further education or a life in missions. Like Michael, Phil thinks deeply about both the issues facing his generation and what it means to follow Christ with integrity as an Xer.

Julie is a writer for a financial institution and also is a volunteer leader with Young Life. She is drawn to teenagers and has an effective ministry with them, in part because of her humility and authenticity. She doesn't like easy answers and is willing to ask hard questions about what it means to follow Christ.

Stacy has had more careers than anyone else on the panel! By training she is an occupational therapist. In the last year she has begun seminary studies and now works on the outreach staff of a church as she pursues a career in vocational ministry. Stacy has remarkable relational skills and an adventuresome spirit, both of which make her well suited for ministry to other Xers.

Sean is the only married member of our panel. Sean and his wife Christine have chosen to relocate to an urban community as they consider a possible future in reconciliation-oriented ministry. Sean is a seminary stu-

dent and works full time as an assistant minister for outreach at a church. He has a bent for and interest in the
arts and is skilled in seeing how the gospel and postmodern culture intersect.

We led the discussion by asking questions pertaining
to the issues raised throughout this book. What follows
are excerpts from the responses of panel members and
some of their interactions.

What is the hardest part of being a Christian?

Sean: Being less self-centered and more centered on
God.

Stacy: Sometimes not getting to do what you want to
do.

Phil: Living out what you are supposed to believe.

Michael: For me, it's living according to what I know
God's values are and what I believe the kingdom is all
about, when there are so many other things pressing in
to distract us. It's difficult because we don't always get
immediate results or immediate pleasure in being a Christian. I know I need to look forward and know that God
has my best in mind and trust that, but sometimes all the
signals tell me that I need to know now. It's hard to keep
your focus on the fact that God's way is the best way.

Who has been the most important person in your spiritual growth and development?

Stacy: I think for me, originally, it was a girl named
Sue. When I was thirteen, she showed me that I could
be a Christian and be normal. She was just cool in my
thirteen-year-old eyes and she didn't read me lists or tell
me things I had to do or become but she just showed
that Jesus was cool and real.

Phil: There was a guy named Drew who was a youth
leader at my friend's church. He wasn't the kind of youth
leader I was used to, who just played volleyball every

week with us. He wanted to talk about God and spiritual stuff. In high school he was one of the few people who really challenged me and made me think about that stuff.

Michael: For me, it was my youth pastor, Nate. One of the things that stood out about him was the fact that he was real about his commitment and his faith. He did what he talked about and when he was faced with situations that were hard, he didn't turn to his own opinions but to the word of God and to prayer. He would challenge me and push me into places that were uncomfortable but he wouldn't judge me. But he would hold me responsible. When I wanted to work as a volunteer with the youth group, for instance, he wanted to make sure that I had dealt with certain issues in my life before he put me in that role.

My mother, too, was very important. What was significant about her was that she was very patient and she exemplified what it meant to wait on God. I went through a time where I really pushed away from God, and she just stood back behind me and prayed for me and supported me. My parents knew everything that I had done and they would express why they disagreed, but they still accepted me and loved me and they didn't treat me any differently.

Who are the most important people in your spiritual life right now? What kind of folks can set the pace for you spiritually?

Sean: I look to people who I feel are beyond where I am. I feel that I pretty much stink at prayer and so I am looking for some guy who is older than I am who knows how to pray. And I'm looking for people who are living in uncommon faith, and their lives are an expression of that. I want to live that way. I want to make sacrifices and I really want to live for Christ but I feel like I need a model sometimes and I'm looking for that kind of person.

184

Julie: I look up to someone who is nurturing and older.

Phil: I would like someone who challenges me in a way that isn't comfortable, who pushes me beyond where I am.

Michael: That was a big part of Nate's relationship with me. Just get in your face and nail you (laughter). And sometimes you'd go home angry. But then it would sink in; he wasn't a patronizer.

Sean talked about uncommon faith. Who are some people you have observed, from a distance, or up close, who seem to have this kind of unusual and vital faith?

Phil: One guy that I meet with every now and then who is kind of a mentor has an uncommon faith in that he is willing to pray for his faith to be tested. In one instance a close family member actually died after he prayed this. He hadn't been praying for that in particular but he had been praying for something that would really test his faith. I thought it was uncommon that he was able to pray for that and then maintain his faith through that experience.

Sean: I admire people who have sold their possessions and given them to the poor. The only two people I know of who have done that are Bill Mallonee, a musician, and Pat Robertson. I don't dial in with anything else that Pat Robertson does in life but I admire that, at some point his faith led him to do that.

Michael: There is an elder at my church who is very involved with intercessory prayer. I wanted to learn to pray and so I went to him for help. Instead of trying to explain how to pray and fast, he said: "Look, just pray!" So the way he led was not to talk about it but to lead a lifestyle of honoring God in that area. I think that's an uncommon thing.

185

What spiritual disciplines do you practice on a regular basis?

Phil: Well, there's always room for improvement, and I hate to use the word *regularly*, but I do try to read God's word and to pray. But prayer is something that the more I do, the less I feel like I know what to do. I am in one of those stages where I find it hard to pray and I go through stages like that with pretty much every discipline.

Stacy: For me, prayer is a big one in two different ways—in solitude and with others. Plain solitude is just a really necessary part of my day. That's not necessarily always a spiritual thing, but solitude is when my mind and spirit usually meet with God. But corporate prayer, too, is becoming important. There's something really different about that. When I'm alone, my mind tends to wander or I think only of the things I am concerned with. But then with other people, prayer gets a whole new, wider dimension.

Sean: I've been thinking about how to be creative with discipline. I read Scripture and pray and fast regularly, but one discipline for me is to leave open the best parking space if I get to work early in the morning. It's just a way to think about the discipline of giving. Now I don't mind taking the second best parking space, for your information!

Julie: I would love solitude if I could ever get it but I don't feel like I get any time alone. I have very limited times alone in my house, because my roommate and I are there a lot at the same time. Also, I'm pretty busy so I'm not there much anyway. Sometimes on Sundays I get an extended time alone but not always. It's just hard to find time and space to be alone.

Phil: For me it's easy to find time to be alone. I'm an introvert by nature and so I enjoy spending time by myself at home, but how high quality that time alone is, that's another question. It's what I do with alone time that is discouraging, not finding the time.

Michael: I'm an extroverted person and I used to shy away from solitude but several years ago I started trying to get alone some. Now I've found it almost addictive.

What are your spiritual gifts, and how did you come to understand them?

Stacy: I've been a Christian for about twelve years and I never really understood what spiritual gifts were. I mean, I thought they were just things like prophecy. It's only in becoming a member of my church two years ago that I had to take an inventory and a light bulb went off. I was working as an occupational therapist, and my top gifts were mercy and exhortation and serving and it was like, "Of course!" That gave me a real sense of freedom that I was doing what God had gifted me to do and that I didn't have to be afraid that I was going to be gifted in some way that I was going to have to do something I hated!

Phil: I've taken two of those tests within the past year and both of them said the same thing, so I pretty much bank on those. They were serving, helping, and teaching and I would have picked those, I think.

Julie: I've never taken one of those tests, actually. But I must fall in the category of affirmation and encouragement. But that's just what I've gathered from my life.

Phil: I think the only problem I have with those kinds of tests is that you can kind of second-guess some of the questions and make them come out how you want them to.

What is most important to you in your friendships?

Sean: The most important thing for me is common ground, looking for somebody who wants to talk about movies and music and stuff that is natural and visceral for me, and to be able to talk and interrupt one another and move to some different direction. To me, that's the joy of life to do that.

Julie: For me, it is just someone you can just laugh with and be yourself with and enjoy life with together.

Phil: A big thing for me is that people are real. Sean talked about enjoying the same things, and that's great but, in terms of friends, I want to know that there's something deeper there. I have a hard time trusting everyone. I need to develop something deeper and to know that they're real about where they stand.

Sean: For me, that pans out in somebody being willing to take time to show they care about me by giving me concrete portions of their time. Something really important in relationships is to meet regularly. I just need that time.

What about conflict in your friendships?

Michael: That comes from being at that level of trust where you know the relationship is deeper than issues. A lot of my friends don't stand where I do on Christianity at all and there's a lot of conflict in terms of opinion, but our relationship is deeper than just thought and opinion.

Julie: Conflict is not easy for me and I don't think that it is a common part of most of my relationships. For me, conflict has always been hurt feelings and a fight.

What is one thing that can most often sabotage friendships?

Phil: Simple things like the pace at which we live and the number of things that we're doing and how much our generation moves and changes. I think it's really hard to keep up friendships and it does take a lot of effort and sometimes I feel like there's a limit and I can't have any more friends. Who of us knows if we're going to be in Charlotte in five more years, you know? And knowing that, sometimes it's hard to really invest in friendships.

Michael: I think it's interesting that what you said about investing in friendships applies to dating too. We're afraid to invest in something that we don't see lasting over a long period of time. And then I look at the root of that and see that it's selfish and that my reason for giving was just to get. And then I think, well, what if I try to go for friendships and just love and invest 100 percent regardless of how long it is going to last, even if it is only for a short period of time.

Let's talk about dating. What's the hardest part about dating?

Michael: I think trust and intimacy, just trusting that person and letting them know where you're coming from and being true with them and telling them parts of yourself, revealing things, letting them see your weaknesses. My biggest fear, actually, is that I'll reveal myself to someone who then changes their mind and backs off.

Phil: I have questioned the focus of dating and I know where I kill myself is trying to figure out God's will for dating. We all know that dating's not talked about in the Bible, but I do think of this in terms of marriage, that God has wired us for that kind of covenant relationship, but I'm so confused as to how to get there.

What did you learn from your parents?

Stacy: I've learned a lot from my parents about reconciliation. My parents struggled in their marriage to the point that we always thought they would get divorced, but when I went to college, they decided not to give in and to go for counseling pretty hard-core. Now they aren't perfect but more at peace than I've ever seen.

So I learned that problems don't go away by giving up. And I also learned that reconciliation is a powerful thing.

Michael: From my father I learned about work ethic, how very important the role of work is, and that he has so much integrity and character. But on the other hand, work can be harmful too, and I don't want to end up in the overwork area. So I definitely have seen that it is valuable to work but I've seen that he can take that too far. From my mother, she has modeled the unconditional love of Christ through her prayer, her diligence in praying for me. She just stuck by me through everything and I can say that my mother has had one of the most significant roles in my life.

Sean: I think my parents were characteristic of others in their generation and parents of our generation, in that they were sometimes too permissive and there were some things I wish they had shut down in my life. There are some things I wish they had made me follow through with.

Julie: Isn't it funny to be able to say that now because, at the time, you would never say that!

Sean: No, of course not!

Julie: My parents were really strict. But they taught me so much about work ethic, my daddy especially, and about integrity. More than anything, they're so loving and are so interested in the details of my life. It just amazes me. They're both Christians, but one thing I didn't learn from them was how to have a relationship with Christ. I never knew what it was like to have a personal relationship with Christ because they're private, very private. But my parents have had the biggest impact on me of anybody, and now I call them when I have to make a decision and I really do weigh what they think.

Sean: My family has given me a lot of good support in terms of encouraging me to have experiences and being very interested in my education. They showed me that they love me by being involved in all that kind of stuff even though they're not very expressive people in terms of expressing affection. I really do value the investments they have made in me.

Michael: When you said that your parents didn't express their love, I just thought how grateful I was that my parents did. My father's parents didn't, and he really makes an extra effort to express love. I guess that you would be more likely to express love in that way because of your family.

Sean: I can easily say it but then, you know, I don't always show it as well. I can feel things and say them but when it comes to being a servant or doing something practical I can be clueless.

You are all involved in some form of Christian community. Tell us something about those communities and why they're important to you.

Michael: I love the fact that it's real. I have some friends who are very antireligion and antichurch and they've come to our community and they see a real place where people aren't saying hi because they want to expand the membership but because they want to know who you are. They care about where you stand. I've also appreciated that we can encourage one another and get excited about God and that it's not just going in and sitting in a pew and hearing a message, but that it's interactive, and there's communication, and people are connecting.

Stacy: For a lot of years, I've been a pretty hard-core individual, and that's been self-imposed. But in the last couple of years here in Charlotte, I've been involved in this thing at my church that is a community for Generation Xers. The value there is affecting our generation with Christ and then *for* Christ, and now I'm moving into that wider thing called the "body of the church" and seeing the value of that wider community. It's been really exciting to be a part of something where there's both older and younger people leading with integrity and being real about failure and struggles, and a community is coming together over questions that no one's quite sure what the answer is, but we move forward and have faith. And the real relationships that come out of that have been powerful for me.

Sean: Part of the realness there is being able to look life in the eye and say that it's tough. That's just really important to me. And something that we say around our ministry is "Life is hard, and if you haven't noticed that, then you're not paying attention."

Stacy: It excites me to see people our age, to see my peers making the right decisions and growing in wholeness.

Sean: We accept in our community that life is hard and that we're broken people, and I think a lot of people come to our ministry from a background where you say "everything's perfect" and if everything's not perfect, then something's wrong. We've seen a lot of people come in and say, "Oh, this is what it's about. It's all about real relationships."

The Discipler's Tool Kit

The Discipler's Tool Kit is a collection of some practical materials to help you in your discipling relationships. The tools are based on the material in the book and are designed to be used flexibly. Some can be used as hand-outs; others may help you organize your thoughts or your discussions. There is not a tool for every topic covered in the book, but the ones we've included may help spur you to develop other practical aids and resources. Be creative.

The Spiritual Timeline

Often a good place to start in discipling relationships is with a spiritual timeline.

Here's how it works:

1. Draw a horizontal line near the bottom of a piece of paper with tick marks that represent each year of your life.
2. Draw a line graph with peaks, valleys, and plateaus all representing your spiritual health at each age.
3. At each high or low point, it might be good to write a brief word or phase that describes what was

going on at that time (e.g., InterVarsity, car accident, doubts).

This is a great way to start discussion, to get to know each other well, and to begin talking about life as a story being told and shaped by a good Storyteller.

Spiritual Disciplines

Practicing Solitude

1. Get away for one hour with Bible and notebook.
2. Get your heart right before God.
3. Read, reflect, listen, write.
4. Focus on listening to God, not talking.

Scripture Reading—Lectio Divina

1. Read a text slowly several times.
2. Meditate on the text.
3. Pray the text.
4. Listen to God.

Practice with Psalm 13:

For the director of music. A psalm of David.

How long, O LORD? Will you forget me forever?
   How long will you hide your face from me?
How long must I wrestle with my thoughts
   and every day have sorrow in my heart?
   How long will my enemy triumph over me?

Look on me and answer, O LORD my God.
   Give light to my eyes, or I will sleep in death;
my enemy will say, "I have overcome him,"
   and my foes will rejoice when I fall.
But I trust in your unfailing love;
   my heart rejoices in your salvation.
I will sing to the LORD, for he has been good to me.

Praying

1. Read and pray through the Psalms, taking up to five per day.
2. Keep a prayer card in your wallet or car. A prayer card is a small card with names of people to pray for. It could also have other words on it that help direct your prayer, like the fruit of the Spirit or the names of places and situations that are on your heart.

Discipline of Fasting

1. It is good to practice fasting in community.
2. It is good to practice it a little at a time (just 24 hours at first).

Sharpen Your Mind

To think well about the culture, we need to sharpen our minds. It seems that Christians are often more *critical spirited* than we are *critical minded*. That is, we are more prone to harsh attack than we are to reflective deliberation and creativity. Roberto Rivera, a fellow with

Prison Fellowship's Wilberforce Forum writes, "We owe the nonbelieving public a little less action and a lot more thought."[1]

The first step in sharpening our minds is to change our approach. We can look for opportunities to tell God's Story instead of searching for proof of the obvious fact that the culture is hostile to the things of God. We can move toward the culture and all its messages without being fearful and self-protective; we can see ourselves as part of a daring rescue mission.

Then we develop a mental filter that intercepts the culture's messages. Many of the messages—and consequently many of the opportunities—fly over us because we do not have our antennae up. While some people are naturally skilled at picking up these messages, most of us need a way to filter the information.

Here is an acronym that may help you create a mental filter that intercepts and evaluates the messages of the culture: TERMS. Ask yourself, *What, if anything, is this saying about:*

T	**T**heology	*The nature of God*
E	**E**thics	*Issues of right and wrong*
R	**R**elationships	*How people relate to each other*
M	**M**ankind	*The nature of man*
S	**S**pirituality	*The nature of spiritual matters*

Theology

Theology is "the knowledge of God." It does not refer simply to scholarly research. While much of the media does not have anything to say about God directly or indirectly, some of it does. We can ask ourselves questions about what we are hearing or seeing. Does this media

196

say anything about the nature of God? If so, how is he viewed? Is he passive or actively involved? Is he silent? Is he good? Is he absent?

Ethics

Ethics is "a system of morals." It refers to what one regards as right or wrong. Often in media, especially in fiction, there are two levels of ethics that need to be considered. The first is the morality expressed by the words and actions of the various characters. That is usually fairly obvious to discern. The second level, however, is harder to pick up.

The second level is the set of beliefs endorsed by the author—the moral stance the author promotes. For example, an author may depict a murderous villain, but it is clear from the tone that she does not wish to advocate the villain's behavior or thinking. In fact the opposite may be true.

However, there are some media in which immorality is considered benign, funny, or even right. Nearly every form of media from novels to songs to movies expresses a moral viewpoint. The central question to ask yourself is, "What is this saying about what is right and wrong?"

Relationships

The culture is packed full of messages about relationships. We hear these ideas on talk shows and soap operas and read about them in novels and magazines. One of the truly sad things about our culture is how distorted our view of relationships has become. Sex is cheapened, marital infidelity is excused, and the abusive use of power has almost become the norm.

197

When these messages are intercepted, ask yourself: "What is this saying about how people should relate to each other?" What relational values are being promoted?

Mankind

"I think he's basically a good person," says the girlfriend of a death row inmate during an interview. A Christian would disagree with such an assessment not because the man committed murder, but because he understands that none of us are truly good. It's interesting that the culture seems fairly split on the issue of the nature of man. Many would say that we are all "good," while many others would say we have a tendency toward evil. Compared to the standard of a perfect God, however, none of us is good—not even the best of us. Watch and listen carefully to the words of the culture. Ask yourself: "What does this say about the nature of man?"

Spirituality

Books about angels, evil spirits, and the afterlife crowd the shelves of bookstores. Movies about reincarnation and demons and returning from the dead play at theaters across the country. Newsmagazines run cover stories on the search for the spiritual. The resurgence in interest in spirituality during the 1990s is both good and bad. Certainly it reflects our culture's yearning for spiritual reality but it also allows an influx of spiritual ideas that may steer many away from God. It is tricky to sort out all of these messages; some of them are deceptive and subtle in their errors. Examine an idea and then ask, "What is this saying about the nature of spiritual matters?"

Spiritual Gifts Inventory

Instructions for Spiritual Gifts Inventory

1. Complete the inventory by using the rating sheet.
2. After you are done, total each row.
3. Look on the definitions page and write the name of the gift in the blank; the definitions are in the same order as the inventory.
4. Circle the gift(s) with the highest rating number(s).
5. Go back and review the individual items associated with those gifts. See how well they seem to match you.
6. Remember that these are only *some* of the spiritual gifts.
7. Also remember that a high score on this inventory does not necessarily ensure that this is your gift. This inventory is merely a guide. It is one of many sources of information for identifying your spiritual gifts.

Some of the Spiritual Gifts

1. *Leadership.* If you have this gift, you have the ability to organize others for ministry. You can probably see both the immediate and long-range goals for a group and can help come up with effective plans for meeting those goals (1 Cor. 12:18).
2. *Compassion.* If you have this gift, you have the ability to feel genuine empathy and deep feelings for those who are suffering or who are in need. Your

care for others moves you to perform deeds that reflect Christ's love and help alleviate suffering or meet needs. This gift is also called mercy (Matt. 5:7; Rom. 12:8).

3. *Discernment.* If you have this gift, you probably have a strong sense of whether or not a person's behavior or teaching is coming from a godly origin. You are able to quickly pick up falsehood or arrogance in others. This gift also allows you to make judgments about what tendencies in your brothers and sisters need to be encouraged or discouraged. You may be able to detect sin or struggle in the lives of others that appears hidden (1 Cor. 12:10; Heb. 5:14; 1 John 4:1).

4. *Evangelism.* If you have this gift, you probably have the ability to share your faith with nonbelievers in ways that cause them to make a commitment to follow Jesus. You are probably comfortable being around nonbelievers and tend to gravitate to places where they hang out (Eph. 4:11).

5. *Exhortation.* If you have this gift, you probably are able to give consistently good encouragement and counsel to others. You probably see an individual's potential and can help encourage him or her toward excellence. You may have a strong desire to strengthen people by helping them resolve problems and move ahead. This gift is also called encouragement (Rom. 12:8; 1 Thess. 2:11–12; 5:14).

6. *Faith.* If you have this gift, you probably have extraordinary faith and trust in God, even in seemingly impossible or tragic circumstances. You have deep faith that God will be in control of circumstances and you see the potential for God to act even in the bleakest of times. Your strong faith is

used to strengthen the faith of others (1 Cor. 12:9; Eph. 2:8; Heb. 11:1).

7. *Giving.* If you have the gift of giving, you probably have a fair amount of money or other material resources and you love to contribute these resources to help support others. You give cheerfully and frequently. You may also give anonymously at times (Rom. 12:8; 2 Cor. 8:3).

8. *Helping.* If you have this gift, you probably enjoy supporting others who are doing ministry by helping to unburden them. You may gladly do practical or menial tasks to help support others. This gift is similar to the gift of serving (1 Cor. 12:28).

9. *Prophecy.* If you have this gift, you probably have a strong desire to call people to repentance. You want people to turn away from their sin and toward God and you don't mind being confrontational to accomplish this (Rom. 12:6; 1 Cor. 12:28; Eph. 4:11).

10. *Teaching.* If you have this gift, you probably can communicate truth to people in ways that they can clearly understand, remember, and apply to their lives (Rom. 12:7; 1 Cor. 12:28; Eph. 4:11).

Rate yourself on these questions using the following scale. Enter the numbers on the rating sheet on page 204.

0 not at all true
1 only slightly true
2 somewhat true
3 mostly true
4 nearly always true
5 always true

1. I am good at organizing groups to do ministry.
2. I feel comfortable being with those who are disabled or in pain.
3. I can tell if someone is trying to cover up an area of sin or struggle.
4. I find it easy to invite people to follow Jesus.
5. I am often asked by other Christians for my guidance or counsel.
6. I can easily see how God is at work, even during tough times.
7. I like to give money to ministries anonymously.
8. I enjoy helping others behind the scenes.
9. I don't hesitate to confront people about their sin.
10. I am good at preparing and presenting a Bible study.
11. I often help organize and manage ministry projects.
12. I feel called to minister to those who are in need or distress.
13. I warn others when I hear off-base teaching.
14. I talk openly with nonbelievers about my relationship with Jesus.
15. I enjoy helping others lay out a plan for becoming better Christian disciples.
16. I can trust God even when the faith of others around me is weak.
17. I believe that giving money to meet material needs is my special ministry.
18. I am often the first one to notice the ordinary needs of others.
19. I don't mind putting up with ridicule if it means sticking up for God.
20. I get deeply troubled when I hear or read some false teaching.
21. I find it easy to delegate responsibility to others.

22. I believe that God chooses me to comfort those who are depressed or discouraged.
23. I can easily identify truth or error when I hear or read the teachings of others.
24. I have led non-Christian friends to a commitment to Jesus.
25. I seem to have the ability to bring out the best in others.
26. I can see God working even in tragic conditions.
27. I often give money for specific needs outside of my church or fellowship group.
28. I enjoy serving others even if I am needed to perform menial tasks.
29. I will confront people who are damaging the reputation of God.
30. I study the Bible well and can share what I find with others.
31. I see the big picture easier than most and I use that insight to provide direction.
32. I feel compassionate for others who don't fit in.
33. I can easily detect spiritual error or false teaching.
34. I enjoy going where non-Christians hang out so I can share my faith with them.
35. I am affirmed for being a good counselor.
36. I enjoy applying God's promises to seemingly impossible or tragic situations.
37. I feel that I should give more than my minimum tithe.
38. I enjoy working in the background to meet the practical needs of others.
39. I don't mind confronting those in authority who are dishonoring God.
40. I don't accept something as true unless I can verify the source.

				Totals	**Gift**
1.____	11.____	21.____	31.____	_____	_____
2.____	12.____	22.____	32.____	_____	_____
3.____	13.____	23.____	33.____	_____	_____
4.____	14.____	24.____	34.____	_____	_____
5.____	15.____	25.____	35.____	_____	_____
6.____	16.____	26.____	36.____	_____	_____
7.____	17.____	27.____	37.____	_____	_____
8.____	18.____	28.____	38.____	_____	_____
9.____	19.____	29.____	39.____	_____	_____
10.____	20.____	30.____	40.____	_____	_____

Thinking about Relationships

In the boxes of the grid write in relationships you have that could be termed acquaintances, buddies, friends, and life friends (see chapter 11).

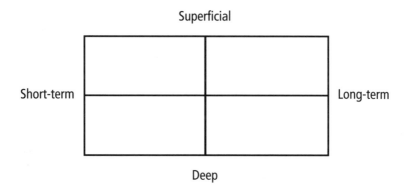

Notes

Preface

1. Douglas Coupland, *Generation X: Tales for an Accelerated Culture* (New York: St. Martin's Press, 1991), 8.

2. Douglas Coupland, *Life after God* (New York: Pocket Books, 1994), 359.

Chapter 1: *A New Hunger and Thirst*

1. Allan Bloom, *The Closing of the American Mind* (New York: Simon and Schuster, 1987), 25.

2. Coupland, *Generation X*, 126.

Chapter 2: *The Story of Our Lives*

1. Leighton Ford, *The Power of Story* (Colorado Springs: NavPress, 1994).

2. Henry Blackaby and Claude King, *Experiencing God* (Nashville: Broadman and Holman, 1994).

3. J. Richard Middleton and Brian J. Walsh, *Truth Is Stranger than It Used to Be* (Downers Grove, Ill.: InterVarsity Press, 1995), 70.

4. Ibid., 77–78.

5. Robert Jenson, "A World Which Has Lost Its Story," *First Things* (October 1993).

Chapter 3: *The Story of the Kingdom*

1. Frederick Buechner, *The Clown in the Belfry* (San Francisco: Harper-Collins, 1992), 165.

2. Tim Stafford, *Knowing the Face of God* (Grand Rapids: Zondervan, 1987), 53.

3. Adam Durwitz, "Mr. Jones," Counting Crows, *August and Everything After*, EMI Blackwood Music, Inc./Jones Falls Music BMI.

4. Buechner, *The Clown in the Belfry*, 153.

Chapter 5: *An Altar to an Unknown God*

1. John D. Woodbridge, "Culture War Casualties: How Warfare Is Hurting the Work of the Church," *Christianity Today* (March 6, 1995).

2. Orson Scott Card, *The Writer's Edge Handbook of Novel Writing* (Cincinnati: Writer's Digest Books, 1992), 45.

Chapter 6: *Eyes, Ears, and Stinky Feet*

1. Kenneth Cain Kinghorn, *Discovering Your Spiritual Gifts: A Personal Inventory Method* (Grand Rapids: Zondervan, 1981).

Chapter 7: *An Awesome God*

1. Stanley J. Grenz, *Revisioning Evangelical Theology* (Colorado Springs: NavPress, 1993), 58.

2. Gordon D. Fee, *Paul, the Spirit, and the People of God* (Peabody, Mass.: Hendrickson, 1996), xv.

Chapter 8: *The Spiritual Disciplines for a New Generation*

1. Alister McGrath, *Evangelicalism and the Future of Christianity* (Downers Grove, Ill.: InterVarsity, 1995), 137.

2. Richard Foster, *Celebration of Discipline* (San Francisco: HarperCollins, 1988).

3. Henri Nouwen, *Reaching Out* (New York: Image, 1975), 21–62.

4. Foster, *Celebration of Discipline*, 96.

5. Richard Foster, *Prayer* (San Francisco: HarperCollins, 1992), 7.

6. Eugene Peterson, *Answering God* (San Francisco: HarperCollins, 1989), 3.

7. Foster, *Celebration of Discipline*, 42.

Chapter 9: *A Reason for Hope*

1. Margot Hornblower, "Great Xpectations," *Time* (June 9, 1997), 66.

2. Ibid., 65.

3. Ibid.

4. Jonathan Edwards, *A Treatise concerning Religious Affections in Three Parts*, vol. 1 of *The Works of Jonathan Edwards* (Banner of Truth Trust, 1990), 234–43. See also Gerald McDermott's excellent modern-day treatment of the affections, which follows Edwards's outline: *Seeing God* (Downers Grove, Ill.: InterVarsity, 1994).

5. The best summary of Newton's thought is found in the teaching of Manhattan pastor Tim Keller at Arrow Leadership Ministries' Advanced Arrow Leadership Program (1997). Tapes are available through Arrow Leadership Ministries, 6230 Fairview Rd., Suite 300, Charlotte, NC 28210, 704-366-8020.

6. Ibid.

Chapter 10: *Family Matters*

1. William J. Bennett, *The Index of Leading Cultural Indicators* (New York: Simon and Schuster, 1994), 44–63.

2. Neil Howe and Bill Strauss, *13th Gen* (New York: Vintage Books, 1993), 55.

3. George Barna, *Baby Busters: The Disillusioned Generation* (Chicago: Moody Press, 1994), 113–14.

4. Kenneth J. Gergen, "The Saturated Family," *The Family Therapy Networker* (Sept./Oct., 1991), 21.

5. Elizabeth Wurtzel, "Parental Guidance Suggested," in *Next: Young American Writers on the New Generation*, ed. Erick Liu (New York: W. W. Norton, 1994), 212.

6. Dieter Zander, "The Gospel for Generation X: Making Room in the Church for 'Busters,'" *Leadership Journal* (spring 1995).

7. Joel Reese, "Dependence Day," *Details* (August 1997), 68.

8. J. I. Packer, *Knowing God* (Downers Grove, Ill.: InterVarsity, 1977), 186.

9. Rose Miller, *From Fear to Freedom: Living as Sons and Daughters of God* (Wheaton, Ill.: Shaw, 1994), 84.

Chapter 11: *Friends for Life*

1. Wayne Lockwood, "God, Where Are You?" *Knight-Ridder* newspapers, November 6, 1995.

Chapter 12: *GenX Sex*

1. Geoffrey T. Holtz, *Welcome to the Jungle: The Why behind "Generation X"* (New York: St. Martin's Press, 1995), 69–72.

2. K. C. Boyles, "No Satisfaction," *Details* (September 1995), 89–90.

Chapter 13: *Building Community*

1. Hornblower, "Great Xpectations," 61.

2. We are grateful to Steve Haas for suggesting the link of the Babel experience and the Jerusalem experience and the implications of this link for understanding community.

Appendix: *The Discipler's Tool Kit*

1. Roberto Rivera, "Mad at the Mouse: Christian Boycotts Are Becoming the Populist Weapon of Choice but Are They Biblical?" *Christianity Today* (February 5, 1996).

Todd Hahn has an M.Div. from Gordon-Conwell Theological Seminary. He is the associate pastor for outreach and new church development at Forest Hill Church in Charlotte, North Carolina. He is author of the study guide for the paperback edition of *Transforming Leadership* by Leighton Ford and of *The Song of the Second Fiddle: The Fine Art of Fellowship*. He is co-author of *Reckless Hope: Understanding and Reaching Baby Busters*.

David Verhaagen has a Ph.D. in psychology from the University of North Carolina-Chapel Hill. He is a child psychologist who consults with several agencies and is an associate with Morrocroft Psychological Group in Charlotte. He is author of several professional journal articles as well as co-author of *Reckless Hope*.